I0142529

KING'S DAUGHTERS TESTIFY

Volume 2

The Power of Pain

By

The Kings Daughters Luncheon Group

Copyright © 2021

R. A. Nelson Publishing

All rights reserved

ISBN: 978-1-637-039-5

All rights reserved. No portion of this book may be reproduced, stored in a retrieval system, or transmitted in any form or by any means – electronic, mechanical, photocopy, recording, scanning, or other – except for brief quotations in critical reviews or articles, without prior written permission of the publisher.

This work may not be copied, sold, or otherwise transferred in any format from one computer to another, through upload to any file-sharing site or software, free or fee-based. Such action is illegal and violates Copyright Law.

The author, publisher, their servants and/or agents accept no responsibility or liability for any such action; the author reserves and retains sole rights to this work.

PIRACY IS THEFT

BIBLE TRANSLATION ABBREVIATION GUIDE:
AMP: Amplified Bible
AMPC Amplified Bible, Classic Edition
ESV: English Standard Version
KJ21: 21st Century King James Version
NKJV: New King James Version
NIV: New International Version
NLT: New Living Translation

King's Daughters Testify

MARJORIE SHULL

My Healing Journey:
God's Faithfulness
Through My DARKEST Night

Many of you are aware of the traumatic season my husband John and I went through when we lost my parents. Many have wondered how I am doing and how I have made it through—how I seem to be doing well so quickly. I have decided to write my story as a testament to God's faithfulness. I am writing this to give God glory for His miraculous work during the DARKEST time of my life, and also to help someone else who might be going through a trying time.

**If you are dealing with a loss,
or anything tragic,
and feel like you can't bear it
any longer . . . hold on.
God will see you through.**

Most of you know that John and I lived with my parents for 2 years and 10 months while being their caregivers. My mama was sick for 15 years, and my father took care of her while dealing with his own health issues. The last several years, my daddy also had a home health care agency coming in a couple times a week to help.

Our caregiving journey began the night of December 25, 2011. John and I visited my parents' house on Christmas morning, as his side of the family would be gathering at Ernest and Mimi's house (John's maternal grandparents) in the evening for our traditional Christmas dinner. While at my parents' house, it was obvious my father wasn't doing well. We were concerned, so we excused ourselves early from the Christmas dinner to return to my parents' house and check on them.

Upon arrival, we discovered my father had injured himself. John bandaged him up, and we decided to spend the night. I stayed awake for as long as physically possible to keep an eye on Daddy, and then I fell out at 3:00 a.m.

On December 26, 2011, I awoke to a representative from the home health agency telling me that she had found my father passed out on the front porch. Guilt immediately began flooding my mind. I thought that if I had just stayed up, I could have prevented this from happening.

The health care representative helped my father into the house. We called 911.

And our journey began . . .

John and I thought that Daddy would only be in the hospital for a couple of days and then be released to go home. We stayed at their house to take care of Mama. Then, we received news from the doctor that Daddy had a case of DKA (Diabetic Ketoacidosis), as well as other complications. The doctor explained that, for my father to live, they had to do a procedure that he may or may not survive. They would have to cut off his breathing for a time. John and I spoke with Mama and released the doctors to do whatever they had to do to save Daddy's life.

What we thought would be a two-day hospital stay turned into three weeks, followed by the news that Daddy could not be released to go home in his condition. The

DKA had affected his mental state to the point that he was unable to function normally or care for himself. My father had to be released to an institution to be rehabilitated and to regain his strength.

I was in shock: in shock at how life had turned on a dime—in shock at seeing how Daddy's health had taken such a rapid turn overnight. He was such a strong, resilient man. How could this be happening? What would it mean for my parents? What would it mean for John and me??

John and I jumped in and started learning how to take care of my parents and their household, while also maintaining our own home. We had NO IDEA what we were getting into. We took over EVERYTHING for them. All we knew to do was pray and talk to anybody who would listen, asking what needed to be done. In July 2012, John and I decided to stop renting our place and move into their house, as we were caring for Mama 24/7 and were never home.

Those 2 years and 10 months proved to be tough and gruesome. I don't think most people *really* understand what goes into being a caregiver. There were scares and close calls with Mama's life, many ER visits and hospitalizations with both parents, dealings with nursing homes . . . on and on and on. There are many stories of red tape, long waits, and—in the end—just wanting what was best for my parents, and wanting everyone whose care they were under to understand that and get on board with us.

Our stress level was through the roof, and it was affecting our health and lives in every way possible. We were completely spent—drained physically, mentally, and emotionally. Our spiritual lives were not in good shape, and we did not have the time that we once did for God or church events, so that connection was not there. I craved worship. There were times when all I wanted to do was scream or escape, but I did NOT want my parents to think they were a burden. I stuffed my emotions and felt like I was not even myself most of the time. We received warnings from some that many marriages in our situation did not last. **We were DETERMINED that this would not be our story.**

In a situation where I didn't think anything positive could come out of it, God was faithful to His promise that all things work together for good for those who love the Lord and are called according to His purpose. **Yes, even in this.** In the midst of all the stress, anxiety, and anger, I was able to talk some things out with Mama privately, and God brought healing to parts of my relationships with both my parents that I don't know if anyone in my family even knew were damaged. It is because of **this** that I am glad I had the opportunity to take care of my parents. Other than wanting to take care of them because they are my parents, it is because of **this** that I chose to do it. I have no regrets.

Almost two years into caring for her at their house, an opportunity opened for Mama to move into the facility at which Daddy was receiving care. Mama requested to be with him.

On June 7, 2014, Mama was in the hospital and not doing well. They did not know what the outcome would be. I didn't tell anyone, but I was secretly hoping that my parents wouldn't pass; I feared that, if they did, I would lose my faith in God completely and walk away from Christianity. I'm part of a church that believes in divine healing. After watching her suffer with illnesses for so many years and not seeing her healed, I had been angry with God and didn't think I could take losing her.

The doctor asked if we wanted to make her a DNR (Do Not Resuscitate) order. I couldn't bear the thought of it. As her power of attorney, if I signed that paper, would it not be the same as me taking her life? I did not want to be responsible for that. My sister, Cindy, explained the situation to Mama, and Mama said, "Do what you think is best." My siblings and I talked about it and spoke to our father, and we agreed to make her a DNR order. My only internal question was, *"When will I have the courage to inform the nurse of our decision?"*

Without communicating to my family where I was going, I left Mama's hospital room and went to the hospital chapel to pray and seek wisdom. I didn't have the strength to talk about it, and I figured my family would understand that I needed time to myself.

When I entered the chapel, I was the only one there. I sat in the front row and—to my surprise—did not cry. I think I was emotionally numb. I simply asked God what I should do. I told Him the family agreed with making her a DNR order, but wouldn't I, in effect, be killing her? I told Him I couldn't do that to Mama. God very lovingly and gently spoke one sentence to me:

"It's okay to let her go."

Immediately, a peace came over me, along with an internal release that it was okay: I would not be harming her. I looked up at the clock on the wall and saw that I had only been there for a couple of minutes. I was thankful that God had answered so quickly. I was thankful for His comfort and peace to see me through.

I left the chapel and returned to Mama's hospital room. As soon as I saw the nurse, I informed her that the family had agreed to make Mama a DNR order.

THAT WAS THE HARDEST DECISION I HAVE EVER MADE.

My family and I decided to go to the house to get some rest. We said our goodbyes to Mama. I said, "I love you, Mama", and she mouthed "I love you" back to me. Those were the last words we would speak to each other on this Earth.

On June 8, 2014, at 10:30 a.m., I received THE call—the one I had been dreading. Mama had passed. I knew she was in Heaven, but I was devastated. I didn't know how to go on without her. I didn't know how to act . . . what to feel . . . what to do. I knew many decisions had to be made, but how would I even have the mental capacity?

All I could do was lie in bed and weep. Every morning I would wake up and cry. Depression set in. There was an outpouring of love and support coming in. I didn't even know what to say to people, or what I needed from anyone. All I could do was mourn. I was in no state to keep up with the house or go to work. I had no desire to do anything. I didn't want the TV on—no radio, no computer . . . nothing. I just wanted to mourn. That was all I could handle for days.

Just when I was starting to feel like I could get more of a handle on my grief, the next call came.

It was twelve days later. On June 20, 2014 at 4:52 p.m., the nursing home called. "We don't know what's going on with your father. Can you come right away?" Something inside me just knew, although I wanted to deny it.

Upon arrival, what I already knew was confirmed. He was gone.

It was like someone pushed the reset button on my grieving process. Both biological parents in twelve days? How could this be?? How would I get through this??? I pretty much isolated myself and grieved for a long period of time. I couldn't function. I had lost both parents. I didn't know how to take it all in and deal with it.

Let me preface this next part by saying that I'm revealing these things because I know that, as humans, we all deal with the same things, and I'm

sharing how God helped me through it. This is not intended to startle anyone.

Losing both of my parents had the opposite effect of what I feared it would have. Rather than losing my faith in God and wanting to get revenge on Him, it SOLIDIFIED my faith. I don't know HOW God did that, but He did. I KNOW that God exists and that Jesus Christ is the healer.

Even though my faith was strengthened, the grief was so deep that I found myself tempted to drink. I've never been a drinker, but the thought crossed my mind to drown the pain and depression by getting plastered. Then, I began having thoughts that the grief was too much to bear and that I didn't want to be here anymore. However, I thought about my husband and how much my family had been through, and I knew I did NOT want to put them through even more pain.

I was surprised by both temptations, but when the suicidal thoughts came, I chose to pull myself out of the depth of grief and depression in which I was drowning. I made the decision that I would NOT allow myself to go that deep into depression again. I spoke to some people and received the help that I needed.

Having dealt with two serious temptations that I didn't want to deal with again, I asked God how in the world I was going to get through this. I knew I could trust Him to see me through it.

God's Supernatural Healing Power

And He did it! On June 8, 2015, the one-year mark of Mama's passing, I was becoming grief-stricken again. I told God that I didn't know what to do, and I asked for His help. I know there is always worship going on in Heaven, so I decided that at 10:23 a.m., the time that she passed, I would have worship music going to join in with what Heaven is always doing.

I put on Kari Jobe's *Majestic* DVD. At 10:23 a.m., the song, "Majestic" was playing. When she sang the line, "How majestic is Your Name", God revealed to me what Mama's entrance into Heaven was like, and what it was like for her to see Jesus for the first time!! I saw Heaven open, and it was a GLORIOUS sight beyond comparison to anything on the Earth!!! Jubilant dancing and celebration!!! COMPLETE joy . . . no pain . . . no sorrow. Not even remembering her illness or the suffering she endured on the Earth.

My heavy grief immediately lifted, and I was happy—happy to know that she is filled with joy, and to feel how ecstatic she was when she saw Jesus. I felt the Holy Spirit infuse supernatural strength into me, and I was able to go on. I was stunned in amazement at God and His supernatural power. I'll always cherish "Majestic" as a song that has a special meaning in my life.

That was the beginning of my supernatural healing process, a healing that only God could do. God was showing Himself strong in my life. What Satan had meant to **absolutely** destroy me, GOD was turning around for His glory!!

Keep the Faith and Don't Give Up

I wanted to share this testimony with you for three reasons. One, to share with you how God is getting me through and how I'm doing so well so quickly.

Second, to say that NO MATTER WHAT Satan throws at you in life, KEEP your faith in Jesus and DO NOT give up under any circumstances. It's by faith that we overcome the world. Without faith, it's impossible to please God. Without faith, we do not have the Armor of God. The Book of Ephesians tells us to put on the FULL Armor of God. Without faith, our armor has holes in it, rendering it useless. Faith is essential to stand against the wiles of Satan and his demonic attacks.

And third, to encourage you that the power of God is real. The Holy Spirit is not weird, and His power is nothing to be feared. We need God's power to make it in this life, especially considering these times we're living in. God's supernatural power gives you the ability to do what you cannot do in your own strength. He can heal you in the broken areas in an instant, where it otherwise would have taken months or even years. All you have to do is believe His Word and receive His gift.

SHANNON BALL

My childhood was not perfect or glamorous, as many would like to believe. My introduction to the Lord was by way of my parents. My father was a military officer, and my mother was a housewife as well as a military wife. If you are wondering why I separated the two, it is because although mother took care of our home, she also had specific responsibilities related to the military as a military wife.

When my father was not deployed, I can remember our family attending church on Sunday mornings and evenings. I can also remember Daddy reading aloud the Word of God. I remember that when Daddy was in Vietnam, he would send ice cream money home to us inside of pieces of paper. This seems perfect, doesn't it? Not for long.

When I was at a very young age, my father was taken home to be with the Lord. Yes, he died, for those who do not understand what that means.

This took place while my father was active duty and we lived on the military installation. Soon thereafter, we would have to move, and our lives would be forever changed. We moved to a house, not a home, where God did not seem to be present. It seemed as if He (God) did not want to be present at all. God was no longer what our lives were centered around. We no longer attended church, and the replacement for God consisted of the ways of the world. This was a very dark time during my childhood.

A few years later, we moved to a home where there seemed to be a faint glimmer of light. Living in the house next door was a military officer and his family. They had a daughter about my age, and we became good friends. The light came from the fact that they attended church regularly on Sunday mornings and Sunday evenings— and they would take me with them! As I look back at that time, I must say, God was letting me know that He was still there with me.

However, this family received orders and moved within two years. I never saw them again after they moved. Another family with two daughters moved into that home, and they also attended church. However, it was not the same. The parents invited me to attend church with their family, but the daughters were not very nice. I struggled with seeing God—seeing the love of Jesus—in either of them! This is when the way I saw the Lord changed. In other words, my view became distorted.

Why Pray?

Now we will move forward into my preteen and teenage years. During this time, there was a spiritual battle (warfare) taking place inside of me. At one time, I believed the Lord to be filled with love, grace, mercy, and forgiveness—for everyone except me. There was a lengthy period during which harsh words were being spoken to me, loneliness was normal, and I kept wondering why I was still here and not in heaven with Daddy. This was the only question I was seeking to have answered.

I could not see that I had a purpose or place. I went through a period when I gave up on God and was positive He had given up on me. I stopped praying altogether. Why would I pray? He wasn't answering, and He didn't care.

Although Mother tried to do the best she could, hardships and struggles seemed to be a way of life for several years. What I realize now is that God used that time to place me on the potter's wheel. (Jeremiah 18:2-3, NIV: *"'Go down to the potter's house, and there I will give you my message.' So I went down to the potter's house, and I saw him working at the wheel."*) He was just placing me there; molding me would come later.

The Husband

Upon completing high school, I went on to college. During this time, I recognized that there was a battle between my spirit and my flesh. I had been taught the Word of God. Yet, loneliness had taken hold of me. I would frequently look around and see what appeared to be happy couples. Many of my friends were getting married. My flesh was longing to belong to a man who would love me, and I would be only his. The only problem was that I chose my husband without seeking the counsel of the Lord.

We met in a jewelry store at the mall. I was there to pick up a key, and he was there with his friend. Both he and his friend were active duty military. We began talking and soon realized that we both enjoyed playing basketball—neither of us being more than people who enjoyed playing and having fun. We agreed to keep in touch and play occasionally. This was the beginning of what I believed would be a lifelong friendship. However, it was actually the beginning of a very difficult and tumultuous relationship that lasted for many years.

Because of my dad, marrying into the military was familiar to me; what I married into, though, was not. Within the first few years of our marriage, we suffered the loss of one of our children. Yet, God blessed me in so many ways throughout it all. It was not until many years later that I could see how He (God) protected and blessed my children and me.

Following the loss of our child, I drew near to God, and God drew me near to Him (James 4:8, NIV). I could hear God's reassurances telling me to have faith, and that He would take care of my children and me. He has kept His promise.

At this point, I was on the wheel with God's hand on me, and the wheel slowly began to turn (Jeremiah 18:5-6). Yes, divorce was the result of me choosing my husband without seeking the counsel of the Lord. However, in the midst of it all, God blessed me with wonderful children.

The Aftermath

During the period when divorce was becoming inevitable, I became fearful of how I would provide for my children. I was also carrying an overwhelming guilt and shame because I had failed. Marriage was supposed to be for a lifetime.

In a great sea of tears one night after my children were in bed, I drifted off to sleep, only to be awakened by what seemed to be a whisper. I heard the whisper tell me, *"I see your tears and feel your pain, and you are not alone, my daughter."* This was when I knew without a doubt that God would take care of us. I turned to God and began to ask, **in the name of Jesus**, for comfort, peace, and provision. (I was more detailed than that, though.)

God put so many godly people in our lives who helped us, prayed with and for us, and—on many occasions—shed tears with me. We have a large family, and those who were aware of our situation surrounded us with love, prayer, and assistance. To assure me, the Lord confirmed that He was at work and in control. On many occasions, the assistance needed was not requested; yet, it was always provided. We were blessed with assistance by God's hand and through His unconditional love for us.

I talked with God one night when the loneliness, shame, sorrow, and guilt from failure seemed to engulf me. Psalm 62:8 (NIV) states *"Trust in him at all times, you people; pour out your hearts to him, for God is our refuge."* So, I poured out my heart to Him. I asked God to be my husband and father to my children. Again, I heard the whisper: *"Raise My sons according to and in My Word, and I will bless you and all of your descendants."*

No mention of the husband part, though!

What About the Husband?

I truly believe God did not mention being my husband because of what He wanted me to decree (state), standing in faith: *"I remain confident of this; I will see the goodness of the Lord in the land of the living."* To accomplish this, I knew—and know now—that I must continue to pray and *"Wait for the Lord; be strong and take heart and wait for the Lord"* (Psalm 27:13-14, NIV).

I believe God will bless me with the man who will love me *"as Christ loved the church and gave himself up for her"* (Ephesians 5:25, NIV). This man, my husband on this earth, will lead me according to God's Word. He will love, protect, respect, and nurture me as we glorify God and advance His kingdom together. Amen!

Glorifying God is the purpose of marriage. Everything else that accompanies the marital relationship (covenant) is and will be added as blessings. "Blessings" means the PERKS, ladies! Don't act like you don't know what I mean.

I will be the perfect helpmate for him

and to him, in every way, according to God's Word. I will honor, respect, and love this man who will strive every day to keep God first in his life. This does not mean a fairytale. Of course, there will be issues along the way. Don't misunderstand: I am not perfect, and I am not praying for the perfect husband. However, I am praying that God will make me the perfect mate (wife) for him.

My remarriage is allowed due to the circumstances of my divorce. However, I prayed and continue to pray that God will fill me with His Holy Spirit and heal my broken areas. I have also prayed that the man God sends me will protect these delicate areas of my heart. We, together as husband and wife, will glorify God, and our union will be such that everyone will see that God Himself brought us together. Thank You, Father!

On many occasions, temptation has been put before me. Ladies, please hear me and understand: if a male professes to be a man of God and tries to convince you to engage in activities that are only allowed within the marital relationship, he is not a godly man! This man is using God and God's Word to promote his own agenda. A godly man's actions will be in line with God's Word. We, sisters, have been adopted into the "royal bloodline" of Jesus. This makes us queens! I have learned that, when we filter what is before us through God's Word, we are able to discern what is truly of our Heavenly Father. Filter, ladies, and be sure you are being respected and treated the way a queen should be treated.

Seeking Provision

Now, on to the specific provisions that I asked God to provide for my children and me. After the divorce, I was in a position where I needed to provide for our family. There was some support from my ex-husband, but not enough for us to survive.

Remember, I asked God for provision. This provision did not immediately come in the way I thought it would. There were several months of waiting before that "still small voice" led me to revise my prayer and be precise about what I was seeking from the

Lord.

I began praying that the Lord would provide me with a job that would allow me to provide financially for our family. However, I asked to work while my children were in school, so I would not be taken away from them for extended periods of time. I was the only parent in their lives, and they needed to have all the love and time God could provide for me to love them, teach them who God is, and show them how much He loves them.

Whew, let me tell you how God showed up and showed out!

God placed an incredible woman in my path who was obedient to Him and opened a door to provide a job in the elementary school my children attended. This meant that my children would ride to school with me every morning. While they were in their classrooms, I would work—and, at the end of the day, we would go home together.

Wait: God was not finished yet! Every day that my children were out of school, I was off from work.

Still not finished, ladies: a few years

later, God opened more doors by turning this job into a career path that provided retirement, medical insurance, sick leave, and paid leave for the days when my children were not in school over the holidays. Hallelujah!

God was at work—and so was the enemy. The enemy was working hard during this time to stop God's blessings. While I was working, taking care of a seriously ill child, and going to school, the enemy kept tormenting me. On many occasions, one particular person was used by the enemy to torment me at work. At first, I truly believed this person was just evil. The fabricating of stories to manipulate others and harm my family, rude remarks, attempts to sabotage me, and unsolicited comments were insufferable. However, God protected my children and me every step of the way—many times, using others to reveal the truth.

One day, in passing, I overheard this person speaking to another co-worker who, on occasion, seemed to be able to maintain this person's behavior and quiet their spirit a little. God wanted me to hear this conversation. I realized that what I saw as evil behavior was actually the result of past hurts that didn't have anything to do with me. This person felt threatened and insecure. Anyone in my position would have received the same behavior. The behavior was due to bitterness, lack of healing, and fear. God allowed me to see this person through His eyes.

This did not change the behavior towards me. The revelation only allowed me to understand and respond in a different way. It would be several years of praying, tears, and wanting to just give up God's blessing before this changed.

Suddenly, one day, this person began to see me differently. I was no longer who they perceived to be a threat. I was the person who would be there to pray for and with them—the person who would help them— the person who loved God. Now, many years later, we greet each other every morning with a "Good morning!" and a smile, both knowing that if either of us should need any assistance at all, the other is there to help. Only God!!

All the tears, praying, and wanting to quit were God creating in me a clean heart, teaching me forgiveness, and continuing to polish my character. Psalm 19:12 (NIV) states: *"But who can discern their own errors? Forgive my hidden faults."* And Jesus states in Matthew 6:14-15 (NIV) that *"'. . . if you forgive other people when they sin against you, your heavenly Father will also forgive you. But if you do not forgive others their sins, your Father will not forgive your sins.'"* I, personally, want to be forgiven.

God showed me that I was to forgive this person—and that it was time to forgive my ex-husband as well. The hurt I was carrying inside of me seemed to be unbearable, and I knew I could only take so much pain before bitterness would begin to take hold. Yet, God revealed to me that this was where my healing would begin.

I couldn't have forgiven both at the same time had it not been for the grace of God! It took many tries before I could muster up the words. Yet, God covered me with grace, mercy, forgiveness, and a blanket of His love. God ever-so-gently reminded me that Jesus forgave and gave His life for those who persecuted and crucified Him. Jesus, the Son of God! By Jesus' obedience and blood, I am forgiven—and so are they. Although they have not asked for forgiveness from me, Luke 6:37 (NIV) states: *"'Do not judge, and you will not be judged. Do not condemn, and you will not be condemned. Forgive, and you will be forgiven.'"* They are forgiven by me, and I am forgiven by God.

See, sisters, forgiving someone whom you believe has sinned against, offended, or wronged you is more for your benefit than theirs. That forgiveness allows God to bless and heal you, as well as send His Holy Spirit to fill you with peace, joy, and comfort.

Every battle is the Lord's, and the victory is His. As long as you have forgiven, this makes the victory yours too. Rest assured, God says that vengeance is His and that He will set the wrongs right. Romans 12:19 (NIV) states: *"Do not take revenge, my dear friends, but leave room for God's wrath, for it is written: 'It is mine to avenge; I will repay,' says the Lord."* All we need to do is be obedient, love Him, and trust Him.

Sisters, I was on the potter's wheel. It was slowly turning. God's hands were on me with His thumbs pressing in, shaping and molding me. During this time in my life, God listened, loved, forgave, comforted, and created character in me that I would never have imagined.

There is so much more I look forward to sharing with you, including many life experiences (revelations) that have already taken place. Others are unfolding at the moment. I will share more with you soon, sisters. Until that time, I pray that God's blessings, favor, grace, and mercy will be upon you. AMEN!!!

LETTIE SHAW

Blessed Assurance

James, my husband of thirteen years at the time (1988), and our two young boys and I lived in Patterson, New Jersey. Our home was a place with a revolving door, my husband's family constantly moving in and out. In 1989, we sold our home and moved to North Carolina because James had been laid off from his job. We also wanted to move closer to family, especially my mother-in-law in South Carolina.

My husband's health began to decline. We would later discover that he had a hereditary disease, Ataxia. Ataxia is a disease that causes the loss of full control of bodily movements. With this deterioration of health, it was evident that he would not be able to work. It was due to this discovery that we began the disability compensation process.

Because I had become the main source of income, my husband and I had to determine what household debts to pay and not to pay. We decided paying the life insurance premiums would no longer be a priority. We were young, and we were not thinking about death or the need for insurance.

However, when we moved closer to family members, my older sister became a thorn in the flesh about the necessity of life insurance for my husband. She asked me what I would do if he died and I had no means to bury him. Yet, my husband and I felt that we were young and really did not need to concern ourselves with life insurance premiums. Surely, his disability would come through, and we would then be on track with our ability to pay our debts.

After my sister's warnings about the importance of life insurance, however, I decided that I needed to at least inquire with our former insurance company. I made the call and scheduled an appointment with the insurance agent. He listened to our story of why we had stopped paying the premiums. He requested additional information. I gathered all the information that he requested, and he discussed our situation with his supervisor. The decision was made by the insurance representative to accept a premium to reactivate our policy, with the stipulation that we would provide an annual medical documentation of my husband's disability. Thank You, Jesus, for favor!

In the meantime, while we were still going through the disability process, we also applied for Medicaid to help with health care for my husband. His health was getting worse, and he was not able to control bodily movement. We were told that my income was too high, and that my husband did not qualify for Medicaid. Yet, without medical insurance, we did not have means for James to get the healthcare he needed.

With great difficulty, we decided to separate so that James could apply and would qualify for Medicaid. We hated that our marriage was sacrificed, but we felt it was the only way to get James the medical help required. It was such a difficult time for our family. The boys no longer had their dad daily, and I no longer had my husband. We separated, but we never divorced. We never even discussed it.

James moved to South Carolina to live

with his mother. He hired an attorney to handle the disability case for him. With much prayer and legal representation, things began to turn around. James was able to see a medical specialist. Finally, we received the medical diagnosis of Ataxia.

James, at last, appeared before the judge to determine his disability qualification. The judge witnessed James' physical condition and his inability to control his bodily movements. Disability compensation was granted for James! Praise be to God for His faithfulness!

James passed away in 2011 at the age of 64. God had blessed us with favor—favor of both God and man—to ensure that we had the means of burying him and benefits to help care for our family.

Through this most difficult season in our lives, we still received God's faithfulness. Hebrews 4:16 reads, "Let us therefore come boldly to the throne of grace, that we may obtain mercy and find grace to help in time of need" (NKJV). We called upon the LORD so many times, and each time, His hand and help were evidently with us. I was so grateful then and remain so still today! Our LORD never tires of His children seeking Him for help in their time of need.

KARI GRACE

I've known Deborah since Deja, her grandbaby. was three or four years old and chose to befriend my youngest, Sara. Yet there are some things Deborah does not know about me. I pray something I share will minister to at least one sister on a deep level. But here's the thing: I don't know any way to be but transparent. I have beauty and flaws, strength and weakness, which is why I need Jesus so desperately. Don't judge me as you read my heart like an open book.

If you're around me very long, you'll find that, sooner or later, I talk about one of two things—perhaps even both: Jesus, and the story. What story? Yours. I am convinced everyone has a tale—but not all are brave enough to tell it. I know from practical experience that writing not only heals the soul of the writer but also all who read, if it's authentic. Maybe it's part of the calling of a writer, but I seem to learn lessons every day—through success, and through missteps.

Including how to survive being raped by a sociopath.

And that dead chickens and wife-swapping usually mean a divorce is coming down the pike.

Today's choices become tomorrow's chains, and my determined purpose is to help others choose to be chained to Jesus and grow way beyond me, in every area.

I'm probably the original "inquiring mind that wants to know". From birth, I've been fascinated by the *why* behind the *what—why* folks do the things they do. People tend to see something or someone and think they know . . . when, in reality, they have no clue. They're judging, but if they knew the *why* behind the *what*, they might not be quite so quick to jump to wrong conclusions based on incomplete—and possibly inaccurate—information.

I have a big *why*. It's the reason I love my Savior so passionately. When you find out at the tender age of 42 that you were born dead and that medical science in the sixties said you'd never survive, it kind of rocks you to your core. Verses like . . .

Then the Lord God formed a man
from the dust of the ground and breathed

into his nostrils the breath of life, and
the man became a living being.
~ Genesis 2:7 (NIV)

"For in him we live and move
and have our being."
~ Acts 17:28a (NIV)

"'I am the vine; you are the branches.
If you remain in me and I in you,
you will bear much fruit;
apart from me you can do nothing.'"
~ John 15:5 (NIV)

. . . take on a whole new meaning.

When you know your own breath doesn't belong to you, the whole stewardship idea becomes a lot more relevant and may even dominate your thinking at times. You totally get that your life—your kids—your spouse—your job—*really* isn't yours. You are content to be thankful for His blessings simply because you understand they are gifts in a very real and tangible way.

Science says human beings are born with only two fears: fear of falling and loud noises. Being the random writer that I am, when I learned that, I made an immediate connection: if that's true, then—logically—*every other fear* is **learned**. Maybe God's onto something when He tells us we need to renew our mind daily. If something is learned, it can be un-learned. But the door you walked through to get into pain is usually the same door you have to walk back through to get out. Most folks would rather accept a lifetime of seemingly little pain (by denial) rather than short-term (possibly intense) pain leading to a free life.

I've always been the kind of gal that looks down the road apiece, because today is not all there is. A classic example of this is seen in the book *Pride and Prejudice*. Two sisters in the same household have a completely different outlook on short-term versus long-term plans and goals.

Fear comes in many different forms, but I encourage you to do some introspective thinking. Are there any fears keeping you from a deeper, closer walk with Jesus? If it's not a fear of loud noises and it's not a fear of falling, you might want to rethink it. I truly only have one fear, and that is the fear of the Lord. Nothing else matters to me. I heard Chuck Swindoll say decades ago, "Hold everything loosely." I didn't understand why that just leaped out of the radio and hit me like a 2-by-4, but now I do. And it all goes back to the stewardship idea. I want to be found faithful when I stand before my Lord.

Choices have a ripple effect, for good and bad. I want to touch folk, impacting lives in this world . . . and the next. That is the primary reason I'm so passionate about writing.

You were created for so much more than sitting on the sidelines, watching the game, never participating—living in fear. You were born with a unique blend of giftings no one else possesses, and a very specific purpose to fulfill. If you use them, you find they energize and fulfill you in a way nothing else docs, propelling you into your calling.

Myles Monroe once said that your book "will go places you'll never go, touch people you'll never meet . . . who wouldn't even like you if they met you." It was the last part that resonated within me. I know I'm a little too energetic for some and I turn them off, but I also know it's my upbeat personality that actually connects me to others. That whole phrase, so casually spoken by a now-dead man, is my biggest dream in a nutshell. He took the words right out of my brain.

Hell is hot and hell is forever, but Heaven's an option too. I want to spend the rest of my life telling folk that, in any and every way possible—including through fiction. I have dedicated my life to doing what other great writers have done: sowing breadcrumbs of the gospel in unassuming stories. Jesus used parables, so I'm doing likewise. And in all the stories I pen, readers with eyes to see, ears to hear, and a heart to perceive may well recognize the Good News. For others, I could just be sowing seeds, trusting they will encounter other Christians who will come along and water those seeds, producing a "come to Jesus" moment of salvation.

Denzel Washington said it's not what you have: it's what you *do* with what you have. We all have so much, but we don't always use it. Who could benefit from your knowledge, your experience, your wisdom? Pay it forward into someone else so they avoid the heartache which mistakes inevitably bring. God has already written every page of your life; Psalm 139:16 says all our days were written before we even showed up on planet earth. I, for one, want to touch every soul He wants me to touch, to do all He asks of me, and to achieve all His plans for me—apparently, through the "foolishness" of fiction.

I choose to live with passion and purpose. Have you found your passion yet? Is it touching folk? Or did you drop it somewhere along the road of life? You can get it back; just ask. When you find your purpose, you'll find your passion, and it will totally revolutionize everything within you and around you. And it will lead you to your destiny.

John Maxwell once said he wanted to be a "people builder and a dream builder." When I heard that I realized: that's something I can give my life to. Frank Peretti said once that he wanted to spend his life handing people bricks, knowing he didn't have to build the whole wall. I can hand people bricks: encouraging words, resources, time, talent, even treasure sometimes. We can all share bricks. The question is, will you?

I like to think of purpose, passion, and destiny as pieces of the jigsaw puzzle of God's individual will for you and only you: why you were born and what you were born to do.

So, what's your purpose? You may know it and be walking in it. If you're not, I believe you know it, deep down inside; you may even think about it often, on some level. So I say, step out and find out! Step out of your comfort zone and see what God does. Stop ignoring it, and start living it. I always say "go big or go home," but you're not me, so perhaps baby steps are all you can handle in the journey towards what you were created to do. Christine Caine says you only ever have here . . . and you only ever have now. I say take a flying leap into the deep dark unknown. What's the worst that can happen? You just might touch the life of a total stranger and change their "now".

Forever. Eternally. Priceless.

"You are our epistle . . .
known and read by all men."
~ 2 Corinthians 3:2 (NKJV)

We are living epistles, read by all.

ROBIN KERSEY

I slowly rolled through the neighborhood again, scanning house numbers. I was frustrated by my inability to locate the address my co-worker had provided. I could not seem to find her apartment number, no matter how many times I drove down the street.

I had promised to visit her that afternoon, and I was not about give up. I presumed I had written it down incorrectly and decided to make another circle around the block. This time I would not focus on the address; instead, I would watch for her.

I was amused, but not totally surprised, when the soldier who had been outside the entire time, tinkering on his car, peered at me with confusion. Had I lived there, I, too, would have stared to see why a strange person kept circling the block slowly and repeatedly. The area had its share of criminal activity. I smiled and waved politely, hoping it would alleviate his concern. He stared at me intently, then resumed his activities under the car hood.

I resumed my slow, measured circling,

peering into yards and doorways, hoping for a glimpse of my friend or her sister. Once again, I had no luck. This time around, however, the soldier had walked out from his car to meet me in the middle of the road. He shrugged his shoulders and mouthed the words, "Are you lost?"

I shook my head, "No," and flashed him what I hoped was a winning smile as the thought passed through my mind that he was probably going to call the police if I continued to circle around his neighborhood. I knew I looked suspicious. As I drove on, a glance in my rearview mirror showed him standing in the middle of the road, hands on his hips, gazing directly into my eyes.

I clenched my teeth in determination and resolved to make one last circle around the neighborhood. I was beyond irritated, and I was concerned that my friend would be upset that I had not known shown up as promised. (Cell phones were not common at the time, and she had no home phone.)

Sure enough, as I circled this time, the soldier had reached the end of his tolerance.

He strode into the road, walking quickly toward my car with no hesitation. This time he waved his hands to flag me down and leaned down toward my car window yelling, "Do you need help?"

I slowed to a stop, and although I felt foolish, I knew I did need help since I had not located my friend's house. He leaned down to my car window, and I reached to roll the window down to see if he could help with the directions. I was embarrassed but smiled cheerfully at his kindness—until I heard a clearly audible voice coming from the empty front passenger seat of my car.

The voice said, calmly and plainly, **"Do NOT open the window."**

I was taken aback; but, being a rebellious sort at the time, I turned to stare at the empty seat and calmly responded, "But I need to find my friend's address, and this man is going to think I'm crazy."

The voice repeated—clearly, calmly, adamantly—**"Do NOT open that window."**

I stared defiantly at the empty passenger seat and said, "I need directions, and he is trying to help"—then reached for the window.

"Don't open the window," I heard again as I extended my hand.

I was actually surprised when the handle would not move. Not to be outdone by an invisible talking passenger, I pushed harder on the handle. By this time, the soldier's nose was about an inch from my window, and we were literally staring into each other's eyes. He shrugged his shoulders and restated that he could help if I needed directions.

I shrugged defeatedly because, despite yet another shove on the handle, my car window would not budge. I spoke back at him through the window, "I can't open the window." He leaned even closer and repeated loudly, "Do you need help?"

I tried once again to move the crank to roll it down, but it would not move in either direction. The invisible voice was silent at this point, but I stared from the empty seat back to the soldier's eyes.

The thought flickered across my mind to open the door and just step out and ask, but it was immediately replaced with another thought that it was probably a good idea to just leave. I smiled weakly at the man, who was still leaning against my car and peering intensely at me. I remember feeling somewhat defeated and very foolish. I again explained that I was unable to open the window, and as he reached toward the handle on my car door, I mouthed, "Sorry! Thanks for trying!" as I waved and drove away.

I went to my friend Deborah's house. As soon as I arrived, before I hopped out of the car to go inside, I could not resist trying to open my car window again. I had never had any problem with it, and the events of the day had me somewhat rattled. The window opened with ease. I rolled it back up, then back down a couple of times just for good measure. It didn't stick, it didn't catch, it required no special effort. It simply rolled down and back up just as it always had. I was confused.

I immediately begin to tell Deborah about the weird experience. I walked her through the chain of events, ending with, "I

KNOW that poor guy thought I was totally crazy. First, I kept driving through his neighborhood in slow motion; and then, when he tried to help, I drove away. There he was, trying to help me, and I didn't roll the window down! I'm not sure he understood why I didn't open it, and he probably thinks I'm just rude."

Deborah stood looking at me in that way that only a true friend will when you are clearly behaving like an idiot, but they love you anyway. She started laughing, and shook her head, and then said to me incredulously, "Robin, you do realize that an invisible voice told you not once, but THREE times, not to open the window, don't you?"

I looked at her, and thought for a minute, and said, "Well, yeah, that's true."

She continued to shake her head in amazement, and said, "Robin, you are the ONLY person I know that would ARGUE with an invisible voice inside an enclosed area where there is clearly no other person present. Then, as if THAT is not enough, when you tried to open the window anyway, it would not open. And instead of you thanking God for sending you an angel, you're worried that some guy thought you were rude. Trust me, my friend, you may never know why that window would not open, but God was with you today."

I thought about it for a minute, and said, "You know, you're probably right. It was very strange, and I was pretty upset because I wanted help with the directions, but there had to be a reason why the voice told me repeatedly not to open that window. Then, it was super strange that it would not open when I tried to open it anyway. Plus, it was working before, and it's working now."

She laughed again and said, "Robin, God loves you, girl, and for some reason He sent an angel your way. Just say, 'Thank you, Lord,' and know that He had you under His protection. If you never know why, just know that He saved you from something today."

I agreed absentmindedly, sat back on the sofa, and turned up the television to listen to the weather.

Moments later, as the weatherman

pointed to the map, I shot up in my seat like a bolt when a picture appeared on the screen where the weather map had been seconds prior. It was the man at my car window! I screamed to Deborah, who had gone into another room to put away laundry.

"It's him! It's him! He's on TV!"

Deborah rushed in to see why I was screaming, and stared at the screen where I was pointing frantically. She looked back at me, and said, "Robin, it's a map."

I turned my eyes back to the television, and the picture had disappeared, replaced with the standard weather map. I was borderline hysterical at this point.

"No, no, no . . ." I stammered insistently. "He was there. The picture was there, and it was him. It was the man who was at my car window. I talked to him. I looked in his eyes. He looked at me. I don't forget people. You know that. It was him! I would recognize him anywhere!"

Deborah looked at me and jokingly said, "Robin, were you out in the sun too much today?" I started to defend my claim, but noticed she was laughing. She knew that despite being "exuberant," I was a pretty rational sort. I reiterated my statement.

"It was him, I tell you! I don't know why they had his picture on the weather report, and I don't know why it disappeared, but they are going to put it back up. I feel it! It was him!"

She walked back into the other room, clearly less certain of my claim than I was. I sat on the edge of my seat, focusing intently on the weather forecast and waiting impatiently. I "knew" he would appear again. I felt it.

My expectations were confirmed when a breaking news alert from Ft. Bragg flashed across the screen. I screamed for Deborah again, this time jumping to my feet expectantly.

"I told you it was him! They said they have breaking news from the base! It's going to be him! You'll see!"

She came back into the room—I think more to pacify me than actually expecting to see this man who I kept insisting was going to appear. We both stared at the breaking news flash and the reporter. As the reporter started to speak about a jointly released statement by Ft. Bragg and the Fayetteville Police Department, a picture popped up on the screen.

It was him. His name was Ronald Gray, according to the caption, and we listened intently as they described how they had just arrested him for rape and murder. Not just one rape and murder—multiple ones. He was a serial killer and rapist. He was an active duty soldier at Ft. Bragg, and as time went on, they confirmed that he picked up most of his victims in the exact area where we had met.

He watched for women who seemed lost or confused, and offered them help.

I felt chills rush through my body. For one of the few times in my life, I was absolutely speechless.

This man who had stood inches from me, looked into my eyes, and offered me help, had intended to rape and murder me. Had it not been for that guardian angel, I would have opened that window without hesitation. I thanked God, and that moment opened my eyes and heart to the reality of the spirit realm that exists beyond the physical world we see. His ways are far above our ways, and His thoughts are far above our thoughts.

Skipping forward more than twenty years to 2017, I had an opportunity to share my experience with a wonderful group of women at my church. The thing that I wanted them—and everyone—to take away from that incident is the wonder and power of our God. We are called to worship Him in spirit and in truth. He tells us in Hosea 6:6: *I don't want your sacrifices—I want your love; I don't want your offerings—I want you to know me.*

He cautions us in Hosea 4:6 (KJ21): *"My people are destroyed for lack of knowledge."*

We must understand that, according to Ephesians 6:12 (KJ21), *"We wrestle not against flesh and blood, but against principalities, against powers, against the rulers of the darkness of this world, against spiritual wickedness in high places."*

We know from 1 Corinthians 13:13 (ESV): *"So now faith, hope, and love abide, these three; but the greatest of these is love."*

Our Father calls us to come to Him for protection and strength and love. He has protected us when we were unaware that we needed protection. He has given us another day, and another opportunity, to live and love and share the good news of salvation. No matter what we think we know, or how much knowledge we acquire in this world, we cannot fathom the wonders that lie beyond what we can see and understand in this physical plane.

We are instructed *to "Trust in the Lord with all thine heart; and lean not unto thine own understanding"* (Proverbs 3:5, KJ21). He tells us this out of love and concern. We are limited in awareness, and while our senses are keenly developed to serve us in this world, there are things happening around us that we don't currently comprehend.

The week after I shared my testimony, seemingly as confirmation, Ronald Gray appeared in the news again. His final appeal was denied, and at the time of this writing, he remains on death row in a military prison.

ASHLEY WILLIAMS

Typing this testimony is very difficult. There are so, so many things I could say, but I feel God leading me to take you along on my journey. I pray my story blesses everyone who reads it.

I grew up under a cloud. I was very depressed. I had seen a lot of hurt and had watched people I loved suffer. I had this negative view of myself that, somehow, I was going through pain because God was angry with me—or that I was not as loved as other people, so I deserved to struggle and hurt. I was a larger girl, and everyone around me made sure I knew it. I felt fat, ugly, stupid, and useless.

Needless to say, I had a tough childhood and adolescence. But, somehow, God allowed me to make it through school, and I decided I wanted to become a doctor—but not for the reasons you are probably thinking. I had watched my family deal with financial issues, health issues, and addiction issues, and I decided I did not want to go through what they had gone through. I wanted to leave my old neighborhood, along with all of the painful memories, and start a new life: one where I could be everything I'd been told I couldn't be.

I pursued this vision and was accepted into my dream college. I thought that everything would be different there—that, finally, I would become this image I had in my head of who I should be: skinny, smart, successful, wealthy, respected. That dream died quickly when I realized I was more alone and more depressed than ever before.

I begged God for a way out. If it meant suicide, I was ready. I even asked God to let me die, but He didn't. The emptiness became so heavy that I tried counseling and medication, but nothing helped. I was in such a dark place, filled with every lie Satan could plant in my head. The thing is, when you are under that type of darkness, the lies of the enemy look VERY true.

My escape was food, and it was my friend. Food was the only thing that did not let me down and was always there for me, so I ate. I also looked for acceptance and love in men, hoping I would find someone who would make me feel all the things I lacked so the void in my heart would be filled. Eventually, towards the end of my last year of college, I met that guy.

Still struggling with depression and medicating with food, I attached myself to my boyfriend. Eventually, we became engaged. I thought that maybe, this time, I could fill that void in my heart; that the depression would finally go away; that somehow, magically, I would become that strong, successful woman I had idolized my entire life.

But it only got darker.

I found myself in an apartment with no immediate prospects for medical school, since I had struggled in undergrad (partly due to the depression). I was engaged, I was a college grad, I had escaped from the old painful memories: I was finally going to start the new life I had wanted for so long. I had everything I thought I needed to live out my dream—my vision of a successful life.

The problem was that nothing in me had ever changed—only my surroundings. I brought all my brokenness, emotional instability, and self-hatred into a new situation. So, again, I found myself begging God to do something—to get me out of this hell. I could not see it at the time, but God had a plan all along.

After that, I began to grow uncomfortable in my situation. I was getting ready to get married, but more and more, I felt this impending sense of doom. I had isolated myself from the few people who did care for me, and I found myself lost, alone, and confused. I knew that something had to change soon, or I would literally lose my sanity—and, possibly, my life.

God was faithful even when I was not following His will. One day, I went to sleep and had a dream. In this dream, I saw myself in the kitchen. I was married, and my future children ran in to hug me, followed by my husband (my fiancé at the time). I will never forget feeling such a deep sense of misery when I saw them.

I woke up frantically, and God said to me: *You have two choices. You can get married, and this will be your life; or, you can follow me.*

In that moment, I knew I would only set

my fiancé and myself up for more pain if we got married, and I knew so clearly what I needed to do. Later on, I had a tough conversation with my fiancé. We broke up, and I eventually moved back home with my family. It was one of the most difficult and embarrassing things I have ever had to do.

After taking a little time to heal, I eventually found a great church and began the process of applying to graduate school. I had hopes of improving my grades to the point where I could apply to medical school. I felt that the cloud of depression was finally starting to lift and that I was in a good place to begin pursuing my dream again. Surely this time I was on the right track to really become the woman I dreamt of being.

I applied to graduate school hopeful, but I was denied by every university. I was lost and confused. I could not understand how I'd finally begun having a real relationship with God but still wasn't able to pursue my dream. I was discouraged and did not know what to do.

Shortly after I received the denial letters, a good friend told me about an internship program at my church based on faith, character, and leadership development. I did not want to do it, but I knew that God was calling me to do exactly that, so I applied and joined the internship. I did not understand how this would help me on my journey in becoming a doctor, but I followed what I knew God was telling me to do.

I completed my year-long internship and, once again, decided to apply to graduate school. This time, I had an open door to some universities—when, out of nowhere, I was presented with an opportunity to work for the internship I had just completed. My heart was torn because I had a dream for my life, but I felt a pull to the internship. I found myself pleading for an answer from God on which way to go, and at the very end of my internship, I heard God say to me so clearly: *I am not finished with you here yet.*

Again, I knew what I needed to do, so I applied for the Internship Coordinator position and was hired. I was excited to begin this new journey in vocational ministry, working with the internship that had changed my life. I poured everything I had into my work; I felt accomplished when I led a successful event; I was determined to be the best coordinator I could be, but God had other plans.

The thing is, I still had this idea in my head of who I was supposed to be. After working in ministry for years, I grew impatient and frustrated with God. He had already called me to lay my dream of being a doctor at the foot of the cross, not knowing if that would ever come to pass; and, while I loved my job, I found some parts of working in ministry—the side that many never see— to be difficult. I experienced many hurts and watched people get hurt. It took a toll, and I began to question if I should walk away completely and pursue my own dream: to go back to school to pursue medicine.

I didn't know following Christ could be so painful at times. But, in the midst, God was taking me on a journey to become who He was calling me to be.

It was at this time that God began to reveal the fact that I did not know my identity in Him, and that I was perfectly created for the purpose He called me to. God began to break the bondage that had kept me in that dark depression for so many years. I began to see myself as the beautiful, intelligent woman He created; that I was not created to be fearful of anything or anyone; that I did not have to be under the bondage of the fear of man; and that Jesus died for my freedom.

Many people accept Christ and have that overwhelming knowledge of God, but never walk in the freedom Christ died for on the cross. Yes, Christ died so our sins could be forgiven, but He also died so that we would live an ABUNDANT life in Him.

So I speak to you today, in October 2017, as the coordinator of the internship program at my church. No, I am not a doctor, and I may never fully understand where God is taking me; my story is, very much, still being written. That being said, I do know this: the past few years have been the most painful, faith-shaking, at times lonely yet beautiful, fulfilling, and joyous years of my life.

Jesus never said following Him would be easy. He tells us to take up our cross and follow Him. But, in following Him, I am finally able to look at myself in the mirror and know I am the daughter of a king, beautiful and prized. I know that my father (God) walks with me even in the darkest moments and works all things to His glory. I know who I am in Christ, and I can write to you today and say that same freedom is available to you if you ask Him to be your savior—your father—your EVERYTHING!

Trust me when I say: it is worth it.

You are worth it!

JOY McNEIL

The Perfectly Packaged Lie

A few weeks ago, I sat in bed thinking about what I could possibly share with you that would be meaningful and lasting. I was on the phone with my friend Ashley, and I said, "There's nothing new to report." I laughed. But, I knew that God would give me something fruitful to share. He always does. He always has. We both agreed that it would have to be an "11:59" testimony, but for some reason, I was so sure the last-minute 11:59 testimony wasn't coming this time.

As I looked around with my natural eyes, my circumstances seemed quite dependable and sturdy. Life was predictable. Until last night, I wasn't truly sure of what my testimony was going to be. After all, I had many topics I could pull from. My life has been dynamic, to say the least. Never a dull moment in any area.

From the outside looking in, it may seem as though I manage to have it all together. I'm 35 now, and on the outside, I've managed to run after all of the things that I thought measured success. Education: I have plenty—enough education to share some with everyone (literally). I've been in school my entire life. I'm a few months away from finishing my doctorate degree; not because I had to, but because I wanted to finish. Yep, I thought it would be a great idea to spend nearly 7 years on this thing.

In the race for a version of success: I have the ideal job of working in the field I've studied for. If you'd like some of my clients, I'd be happy to share those too. After all, I don't have to watch reality TV—honey, I don't even have to see the news, because what I experience every day as a mental health clinician blows my mind. I literally go home breathless every night after hearing and seeing the prison that some families live in daily. It has taken hearty faith not to crumble under the weight of the boulders they bring into the office.

But, back to the appearance of success: I lived out the lyrics of the old Destiny Child song which said, "All my independent women, throw your hands up at me." Get out there—get yours, girl—go for it! There's another song that says, "She got her own flat screen." Yep, I got that too. Because we are in the business of appearing as if we have it all together and figured out. Neatly pressed, cute shoes, blinged up, perfect pose and smile, camera-ready—but hiding the bruises, the breaks, the dirt, and the shame. Perfectly packaged.

Let me say that again: We are neatly pressed, blinged up, camera-ready on the outside—and bleeding on the inside. We're hiding the bruises, the breaks, the dirt, and the shame.

In sharing about my story, I could talk to you about my 24-year-old self who was happily living in D.C.: in her own place, with her own job, working for a lobbyist with the Lupus Foundation of America, traipsing up and down the halls of the Capitol, on the phone with congressional leaders, and finally doing it big. Then, I suddenly began to get sick, had a seizure, and ended up in the hospital.

The night before I got sick, my boyfriend at the time was over at my home, living it up. I thought I was big-time: playing house, having sex, enjoying pleasure, being young and professional and in the city—but dying inside. There was something wrong with my body. It was peculiar, but I pushed it to the back of my mind because I was living the perfectly packaged lie.

The next day, after a night of what I thought was growing love, I woke up in the hospital. I was diagnosed with systemic lupus—an autoimmune disorder in which the body begins to attack itself. But, in the midst of the weird, oppressive feeling that my life as I knew it was over, all I wondered was, "Well, where's my boyfriend"? Day One in the hospital: my boyfriend broke up with me over the phone. I'll never forget that phone, because it was a phone outside of my hospital room. I had to walk to it. He told me he was done with me. I spent two weeks in that hospital, trying in vain to go back to the perfectly packaged lie.

In sharing my story, I could share extensively about my 4-year abusive relationship with a man who I would later find out was married. He seemed to live effortlessly in two worlds, always coming sideways and never straight to the point. I was 27 and still rather young and naïve, so I bought his perfectly packaged lie and thought he was the perfect man for me. Never mind the fact that I constantly looked over my shoulder, feared for my safety, and couldn't predict when he would show up at my home. Never mind the games, the lies, and the disappearing acts. He would give affection and take it away. He would get nasty and turn sweet. His goal was to keep me hanging on, and I did that well. I hung in there like a champ, and even when I found out his true identity, I hung in there because his words and ways were like a sweet poison: killing my soul, but making love to my flesh.

It took nearly an act of Congress to finally break us up. Maybe it was his gun at the bottom of my staircase after yet another fight. I wasn't sure if he was planning to take my life and then his own. Or maybe it was him threatening my job. Perhaps it was him moving in with me briefly and causing me so much chaos that I actually called friends and said "If anything happens to me, it's ok. I know that I probably won't make it out of this." The relationship was a devil, and I didn't have the tools for battle. I was stuck. I almost didn't make it out alive, but I made it, and so did he.

At that point, nearly 30, I had begun a journey away from the perfectly packaged lie. That's not God's best. When we are living in sin, unrepentant and even refusing to acknowledge the sin, we lose the ability to really see and press through on our way. That's what the enemy wants.

Last but not least, earlier this week, I was going to share about how all of my past junk led me down a path towards reluctant leadership. God has placed in my soul a fire to see women, particularly single women—of which I am a bona fide, platinum card-carrying member—break free of the chains binding them. After all, I had my own collection of perfectly packaged lies; God was bringing me out of my stuff, and He asked me to pull others along too. That's how I started the small group BRAVE Diva: Bold Righteous Authentic Victorious Extraordinary Diva in Christ. I knew it was time for women to get out of bed with Mr.

Wrong, to get out of sometime-y relationships, to get out of the victim mentality, to get out of being a doormat—to get out of settling for anything less than God's best. It was time for newness in Christ, and I was passionate for a change.

However, in many ways, I have been a reluctant leader, trying to find my voice in the midst of turmoil. I had an overwhelming desire to hide in the back, or to run from destiny rather than embracing it. Truth be told, I would really rather go my own way on some days. When it's hard, and when I don't feel I have the juice for another minute, there's no amount of Joyce Meyer preaching, Manna teaching, or positive connections in the world that can reach me. I honestly want to hide—and hide well—behind familiar walls that we normally build to keep everyone out.

I read an interesting quote on reluctant leadership by David Brooks of *The New York Times* (2014):

"The Bible is filled with reluctant leaders, people who did not choose power but were chosen for it. . . . The Bible makes it clear

that leadership is unpredictable: that the most powerful people often don't get to choose what they themselves will do. Circumstances thrust certain responsibilities upon them, and they have no choice but to take up their assignment."

When God was passing out assignments, especially on this mission of life, I can't say that I was ready to take up mine with gladness. I was excited to bring together women, single women in particular, and grow closer in Him—but there was comfort in the perfectly packaged life of old. There was familiarity in hiding and staying out of the limelight.

Because the very moment I decided to step into women's ministry fully, with my whole heart, the attacks came full on. The headaches, the eye pressure, the lupus starting to flare out of control, the mental anguish, the conflict, the drama . . . *Wait, God; wait. I'm reluctant to stay at this post because this is not what my assignment was supposed to be. I've been fighting. I've seen fighting. And, now, I'm supposed to lead this fight? Lord, when you were passing out assignments, perhaps you gave me the wrong person's paper!*

And this is where my story picks up.

Let me remind you, sister, where we've been, in case you've lost me: two weeks ago, I said I really didn't have a testimony to share for this gathering today, because my circumstances seemed quite normal in the natural. I had a bunch of stories I could share about battles in my past, from lupus to broken relationships, until I settled upon the topic of reluctant leadership earlier this week.

I found that leadership meant taking enormous hits, and I honestly did not want the beating. I didn't want the responsibility. And yes, BRAVE Diva—the not-so-small small group—was very blessed, but I felt an even deeper calling in my spirit that required explanation. Plus, I felt the weight of the call so heavily that I had to step away for a moment to catch my breath. I was weary. I did not want the weight. But neither did I want to go back to the perfectly packaged lie.

I am in the midst of a great transition in

my life—a shift, if you will. I am soon to be finished with my doctoral dissertation, and after a pause, I have decided—reluctantly at times—to step back out again and further my assignment. I am co-leading a singles group for the 30+ crowd, because I want the world to know that we are not forgotten. There's nothing wrong with us. If you want to help us, you can pray for us, encourage us, lift us up, and connect us with other people who seek God. The days of singles-shaming must cease. God has a purpose for each and every person—each and every single, each and every one—and we need to stop sweeping singles under the rug as if they are a problem that needs to go away.

I don't hear anyone talking about the fight for purity—the fight for holiness in a world of full of hellishness. I don't hear anyone talking about how to mentor the single women and men out here; this world is a dirty place, and we have to fight against the world's way every day. We are in the world, not of it. We have an intercessory prayer group that meets monthly to lift up singles and marriage and godly purpose, because God has not forgotten about you.

Stop suffering in secret, trying to figure it out on your own. In this season, God is saying, *"Baby, YOU DON'T HAVE TO FIGURE IT OUT."* You need to stand in Christ, no matter how many people come into your life. You may feel reluctant, like me, at times—but sister, you have got to get armed up and get into the fight. The thief wants to sift you like wheat, and you're lying down for him, ready to be sifted. No! Get up!

Speaking of prayer and faith and believing God, this week I met someone who appeared to meet my criteria for a shot at the title. He said all of the right things. He was handsome and suave. He was funny. He and I shared similar values, and he came saying many of the things that I wanted to hear. He wanted to do things the traditional way. He was interested in getting to know me and pursuing me correctly. We were going to seek God together. A praying man, it seemed. Full of determination. Full of promise. As the week went on, we saw each other every day, talked for hours, and went out on 4 or 5 dates. It seemed to be going well, in that we had laid all our cards out on the table, and we set about the process of getting to know each other.

There was one thing missing. He was in-between churches, so I invited him to come to church on two occasions. His spirit seemed to shut down, and he distanced himself from me. In this moment my own thoughts began to wear me down . . .

This takes me back to a quote in *Fervent* by Priscilla Shirer: *"If I were your enemy, I'd tempt you toward certain sins, making you believe that they are basically (even biologically) unavoidable. I would study your tendencies and proclivities until I learned the precise conditions that make you the most likely to indulge them. And I would strike right there. Again and again. Wear you down. Because if I can't separate you from God forever, at least I can set you at odds with Him for the time being."*

You see, the enemy is great at recycling and repackaging the same old dirt to make it look brand new. The enemy studied me, and he knew what I normally liked and disliked. The thing is that I know he knows, and I know enough to know 1 John 4—"test every spirit," as my friend graciously points out in the Word. While this guy may have said he wanted to get married and have a powerful relationship, his actions did not line up. Once he realized that I wasn't a "typical church girl" (whatever that means), that spirit had to bounce.

He was over at my home, and I remember that night well, because I was terribly tired from a harrowing day at work. He'd had a rough day too, and so out of the compassion in my soul, I decided to cook up something. In the midst of exhaustion, I stayed true to my God by not placing myself in a compromising situation. No worries. We did not touch except to hold hands in prayer. Well, when it was time for him to leave, he begged to stay and refused to leave. He outright refused to leave. It took me 45 minutes to get him to leave my home. I felt myself getting angry: "Dude, it's time for you to go."

A day after I finally got him to go, he stopped wanting to talk as much. By Friday, he was posting sexually explicit comments on another person's Facebook status messages. As I learned more and more about him, I realized that the façade—the perfectly packaged lie—was in play. And, as of 11 p.m. last night, I had another testimony—and yes, it was an 11:59 testimony. For you see, the assignment God placed on my life caused Satan to get busy packaging and repackaging the same dude in a different body to trip me up and keep me off focus. To keep me out of control, out of sync, and off-course.

Needless to say, I deleted the man on social media, and I ended our connection. But my war isn't really with him.

Fervent by Priscilla Shirer goes on to state, *"If I were your real enemy, I'd disguise myself and manipulate your perspectives so that you'd focus on the wrong culprit—your husband, your friend, your hurt, your finances, anything or anyone except me. Because when you zero in on the most convenient, obvious places to strike back against your problems, you get the impression that you're fighting for something. Even though all you're really doing is just fighting. For nothing."*

So last night, I had to go to war again. Not against a person—that's where we get it wrong. It's a spirit. It's a perspective. It's an unhealthy thought-pattern and belief. It's a perfectly packaged lie. Some of us have invested in the lie. Or we've fought the person instead of focusing on the real enemy.

Remember this:

- *Satan is determined.*
- *Satan is determined to block your spiritual inheritance.*
- *He is determined to destroy mindsets and distract your thoughts.*
- *He is determined to make you hate yourself—to loathe your season—to be uncomfortable with spiritual things.*
- *He doesn't want you to get married.*
- *He doesn't want you to meet a godly mate.*
- *He wants you bound.*
- *He wants you broken and sifted like wheat.*

- *Just when you think you are having a breakthrough, he attempts to send a breakdown.*
- *He wants you overwhelmed.*
- *He wants your underachievement.*
- *He wants your disillusionment.*
- *He wants your destiny.*

Listen, my sister: the enemy never comes head-on for you. He comes in the form of bittersweet relationships and of situations that make you settle. He comes in the dead of night when you're lonely and vulnerable. He comes when you're at your lowest—and your highest, when you're operating in your fleshly strength. He comes in the form of pride whenever you refuse to ask for help. He comes in the form of worldly things that seem ok at the time but are really traps. He comes in the form of ideas that sound completely rational, yet are completely false. He is determined, and he never sleeps, and his minions never sleep, and he is gonna keep coming—whether directly or indirectly—until he has finished the task of destroying not only you, but your bloodline.

We must be determined to be permanently bonded to the things of our Lord.

To strap up our warrior boots.

To get rid of the quest for perfection and get into our godly purpose with joy.

Stop investing in the dirt of yesterday, and start presenting those wounds and cleaning them out.

Over the course of this week, the Holy Spirit reminded me of the parable of the 10 bridesmaids in Matthew 25 (NLT):

"Then the Kingdom of Heaven will be like ten bridesmaids who took their lamps and went to meet the bridegroom. Five of them were foolish, and five were wise. The five who were foolish didn't take enough olive oil for their lamps, but the other five were wise enough to take along extra oil. When the bridegroom was delayed, they all became drowsy and fell asleep.

"At midnight they were roused by the shout, 'Look, the bridegroom is coming! Come out and meet him!'

"All the bridesmaids got up and prepared their lamps. Then the five foolish

ones asked the others, 'Please give us some of your oil because our lamps are going out.'

"But the others replied, 'We don't have enough for all of us. Go to a shop and buy some for yourselves.'

"But while they were gone to buy oil, the bridegroom came. Then those who were ready went in with him to the marriage feast, and the door was locked. Later, when the other five bridesmaids returned, they stood outside, calling, 'Lord! Lord! Open the door for us!'

"But he called back, 'Believe me, I don't know you!'

"So you, too, must keep watch! For you do not know the day or hour of my return."

Be so determined that you do not allow your light to grow dim by chasing after what you think you need. It's time to let go of the perfectly packaged lie and keep on fighting for what's good, what's lovely, what's honorable, what's pure, what's admirable.

Sister, if you're not prepared, it's time to get prepared. It's time to get your oil, to not go to sleep, and to not get weary of prayer or of doing good. Please do not drop your armor when it gets heavy.

Yes, you might be reluctant like me, but stay at the ready. Wear your Bible out. Get someone to be your accountability partner. Because honey, in this fight, we WIN—but you can't keep selling yourself out to the perfectly packaged lie. Keep your lamp lit. I don't have this thing figured out, but I know that Jesus is my Lord, and my Lord leads me to a life that is greater than any perfectly packaged existence I could ever conjure for myself.

Initially, "Relationship Rules" was a post about rules for being single and not settling:

She's single because . . .

she refused to change her relationship status for someone who falls short of what she deserves.

she knows her value.

she's chosen to preserve a spot in her heart for a real man, someone mature enough to understand that loyalty, commitment, and honesty are priorities and not options.

And she will wait . . .

In the season I'm in, I had to change it a little bit:

She's a single Daughter of the King, and she fearlessly refuses to settle for less than God's best in any situation at any time.

She's chosen by the King and perfectly kept for the assignment He created her to live out boldly on the earth.

She has chosen to wait upon the Lord for a man after God's own heart, not after success in the standard of the world: someone who's not faking this walk, or just talking the talk, but living it out day to day, come what may.

She's done settling and compromising for scraps under the table.

She is not a doormat; she is a WARRIOR, and she is fiercely wielding her sword of truth in battle.

And she will pray, and she will war, and she will not let her lamp go out while waiting on the King of Glory to come in.

She is FIERCELY AWAKE. A woman of faith. Not perfectly packaged—BUT

PURPOSED FOR THE GOD-DESIGNED GREATNESS WITHIN HER.

Please don't fall asleep and let your lamps go out. We need you fully awake—locked, loaded, and ready. Sister, I write this fully aware and fully awake now. Before, I seemed to fall for cycle after cycle of the perfectly packaged lie. And now, I'm more prepared, more passionate, more prayerful, more powerful, and more at peace, passing the packages of lies on by. I pray the same for you. God wants all of you, fully and completely. No lies. Only truth and love—and you can count on it.

Join me in this freedom.

DEBORAH SHEPHARD

God Is a Healer

"But He was wounded for our transgressions; He was bruised for our iniquities. The chastisement of our peace was upon Him, and with His stripes we are healed."
~ Isaiah 53:5 (KJ21)

How many of you know that God is a healer? I know that He is a healer and a deliverer. That is why this scripture means so much to me.

Today I would like to share testimonies about how God healed me and why I trust Him.

When I was about 25 years old, my adversary—Satan himself—tried to afflict my body. I was dealing with an "issue of blood", and it seemed as if this issue would present itself every Sunday when I was at church singing in the choir. I finally decided that I needed to seek medical attention so the doctor could make a diagnosis and I would know what my affliction was.

I went to the ER at Schofield Barracks and briefed them concerning my symptoms. They kept interrogating me, trying to determine if I was having this issue of blood because of my menstrual cycle. I explained to them that this was not the problem, so they finally decided to do a catheterization. After the catheterization, they realized I was correct. They could not make a diagnosis, so they scheduled an appointment for me to go to Tripler Hospital to have a test done. Based on the symptoms I described, they thought I was trying to pass some kidney stones, so they wanted me to have an IVP (an X-ray to look at my kidneys, bladder, and urethra).

I had the test done, but I never received a phone call or any information concerning the results of the test. I called the lab at Tripler and was informed that the results from the IVP were negative and that the tests did not reveal anything.

Well, what do you know? I was still having the same issue. Guess what I did! I decided to have a little talk with my Heavenly Father, the Great Physician. I began to pour out my heart to God: *"Lord, you are my Creator, and you know all about me. You knew me when I was in my mother's womb. There is an affliction that is attacking my body. I am coming to you, Lord, because man is astounded by the fact that they can't determine why I am dealing with this 'issue of blood'. You are omnipotent and omniscient. You have all power in your hand, and you know all. I need a touch from the Great Physician, my Healer! Lay your hands on your daughter, that I might be made well!"*

Well, to my amazement, I realized a few days later that I was not having those symptoms anymore. After I sought the Lord and poured out my heart to Him, my problem was resolved. God had touched my body, and He had made me whole. This was enough to convince me that my God is real: He is a Healer! I now know for myself that God truly was wounded for my transgressions; He was bruised for my iniquities; the chastisement for my peace was upon Him; and, by His stripes, I was healed.

How many of you know that Satan will present himself again? Mind you, they thought I was having my menstrual cycle when I was dealing with the "issue of blood". Well, suddenly, I was not having my cycle. This went on for four months before I finally went to the doctor to try to determine what was going on. Of course, the doctor thought I was pregnant, so I had to take a pregnancy test. The pregnancy test was negative, so the doctor prescribed me some medication that would cause my cycle to recur.

When I got home and read the side effects of the medication I had been prescribed, I decided that I was not going to take the medication. I felt the medication would cause more harm than good; one side effect was that it caused tumors. I had another talk with the Almighty God about my situation, and what do you know? God touched my body again!!! This is why I love Him so!!! He healed my body again, and I've never dealt with that issue since.

Can you believe, though, that I had another issue pertaining to blood? About 10 years ago, I was admitted into the hospital because my blood was low. I was anemic. When the doctors received the results from my blood work, my hematocrit was 7 and my hemoglobin was 7. They said, "We don't know how you walked in here; your hematocrit and hemoglobin are half what they should be. We need to keep you overnight so we can determine why you are losing so much blood. We need to rule out cancer. You are going to need a blood transfusion, because the iron pills will not be sufficient due to the severity of your iron deficiency.

They took me down to have an ultrasound done, then they brought me back to my room. I began to talk to the Lord about the blood transfusion. I said, *"Lord, if I have a blood transfusion, let it be the blood of Jesus."*

As I was lying on my bed at the hospital, it felt like somebody shook my bed. I thought to myself, *"There is nobody in this room with me."* I looked up, and there was nobody in the room with me. I closed my eyes again, and I felt the same shaking of the bed. I opened my eyes, and again, there was nobody at the foot of my bed.

I then heard a still, small voice: *"It is well, all is well."*

I did not have a blood transfusion, and I did not have cancer. They did prescribe me some iron pills, but how many of you know that I don't do well with pills of any kind. I stand to report to you today that I am not anemic. God healed me again. God is a healer! Can't nobody do me like Jesus!

Just a few weeks ago, I was scheduled for cataract surgery. On Oct. 9, I went in for an evaluation, and they administered several tests that were about two hours long. Prior to the tests, I had communicated with my Heavenly Father about this issue as well. *"Lord, I don't want anybody operating on my eyes. Lord, I need you to do a surgery without hands."*

I saw God's divine intervention again. After the doctor looked at the results of the test, he said, "I love my job and I have been doing this for years, but I don't recommend you having this surgery. Yes, you have a cataract, but we all get them as we get older. They may be a little inconvenient at times, but not enough for you to have the surgery. There is a zero percent chance of any complications, but any surgery is major. If you don't have the surgery, there is no chance of anything going wrong."

I said, "So you are recommending that I don't have the surgery?"

His response: "Exactly!"

Lord, I thank you again!

I got home and began to reflect on the conversation I had with the Almighty God concerning the surgery on my eyes. I know it is not just in my mind: since that appointment, I have not felt that cataract, and it does not affect my vision.

God is a healer! Trust Him! There is nothing too hard for God. All things are possible if we only believe. Faith is the key! Faith without works is dead. We must believe that He rewards those who diligently seek Him.

"Heal me, oh Lord, and I shall be healed; save me, and I shall be saved . . ."
~ Jeremiah 17:14 (KJ21)

God has healed me even when I was

broken, when I was wounded, and when I was in despair. I know that God will mend up the broken heart and that He will deliver you out of all your troubles. God will heal you physically, spiritually, and mentally if you allow Him to. God is a healer!!!!

AERIYA GRIFFIN

I would like to say a prayer:

Father God, I thank you that we are fearfully and wonderfully made in Christ Jesus. I pray that you would release your power and glory in this place and that you would release your angels. I pray in the name of Jesus that you will anoint my testimony, and that as others give their testimonies, I pray that you would anoint their testimony also, in the name of Jesus. I speak a blessing of peace, love, and a sound mind. I bind any spirt of rebellion and doubt that would try to destroy our faith and relationship with you. I pray that you would set the tone of the atmosphere as I give my testimony. In the name of Jesus, Amen.

My testimony starts with my mother. She grew up with no father or mother around. She made poor decisions. I was born out of wedlock. When my father found out that my mother was pregnant with me, he asked her to abort me, because he already had many kids and could not support or take care of them. My mom refused to abort me and decided to keep me and raise me.

As a young single mother, my mom was depressed and far from God. She struggled to take care of me until she met the Lord, and decided to dedicate me to Him, in 2009. We started going to church and built relationships with people. We also did a lot of community service, because we knew that we were blessed, and we wanted to help others see the love and grace of God.

We did prayer walks with our church; being young and chubby, I liked the prayer, but I did not like the walks. We also started to feed the homeless—the place where we would serve was called Loaves and Fishes. I loved it, especially when the people showed up and we had to hurry, placing food on the plates and giving it to them. That's what I called "rush hours". Like I said, I was chubby, and I loved me some sweets. The head of Loaves and Fishes always gave me some candy or cookies after we served. Unfortunately, the head of Loaves and Fishes died due to health problems, but I know she touched a lot of people's hearts.

When I was in elementary school, from

about 1st to 4th grade, people would speak things over me, saying that I could not comprehend well. I was also having many issues in school with my grades. One reason was that I was a chatterbox, so that's why I kept getting in trouble. But my mom would not let them speak such things over me, and she would always say, "I bind that in the name of Jesus." She would hang words of affirmation on my bathroom mirror to say to myself every morning.

As I was coming of age, my mom would not let me watch, listen to, and be around certain things. There are many things that are not good for your spirit if you watch or listen to them, such as horror movies, shows with sexual activity, and certain types of music.

When I was in elementary school, my mom would take me to see my dad, but he would never make an effort to see me. Not having a relationship with my earthly father allowed me to realize that I had the spirit of rejection. It was clear in my actions that I was not confident in myself or in my relationships with others. I was extremely shy and not confident, so when I walked, my shoulders were hunched and my head was down.

However, it says in John 15:16 (NLT): *"'You didn't choose me. I chose you. I appointed you to go and produce lasting fruit, so that the Father will give you whatever you ask for, using my name.'"*

I may have been a surprise to my parents, but I was not a surprise to God. It may be true that my earthly father did not try to get to know me, but my heavenly Father knows me. I know that God has chosen me for a greater purpose in life, and that He has created me in His own image. I have been told that I am an intercessor, standing in the gap for people and praying.

God turned it around for me: I am now in Honors Literature, and I have a full understanding of my work. I strive to get outstanding grades because I try to do things with a spirit of excellence. (Plus, if I don't get good grades, I would be feeling down—especially because I would get a lot of lectures. Since I already get a lot, I can't take anymore.) I am currently tutoring my cousin in math, and his grade has gone up a lot.

Christ has helped me accomplish many things. I have passing grades because of Gods glory. I no longer have to hold my head down or try to change my personality for others and live a life of duality. Instead, I know that I am found in Christ.

So, even if you feel like no one understands you or like you're all alone, God is there for you and understands your pain. Always remember that others do not define you—God does.

"Now to him who is able to do far more abundantly than all that we ask or think, according to the power at work within us, to him be glory in the church and in Christ Jesus throughout all generations, forever and ever. Amen."
~ Ephesians 3:20-21 (ESV)

Thank you all for listening with open minds and hearts.

NICY BISHOP

From the Eyes of a Child to the Heart of a Woman

The Peacefulness of Knowing

She was a beautiful woman—a tiny little thing, all of 4 feet 9 inches. Even with a myriad of health issues, she looked 60 or maybe 65; regardless, she looked much younger than her 75 years.

Sitting up in bed, in her elegantly decorated nursing home room, she looked at me thoughtfully.

"Nanoune," she started, "I got a call yesterday that my good friend died in Haiti. We went to nursing school together."

"I'm so sorry to hear that, Mom. Were you two close?"

"We were," she replied, a bit misty-eyed. I held her hand for several moments before she spoke again.

"Nicy?"

My mom rarely called me by my given name, so I knew this was important.

"Yes, Mom?" I answered, watching her.

"I don't understand why, year after year, God allows my friends to die and leaves me here still. Why can't I die? I want to die! Is it wrong for me to want to die?"

I smiled at her, knowing the things she had endured just in the past few years.

"No, ma'am! It's not wrong for you to want to go be with the Lord!"

A smiled played across her lips.

"I have lived and loved the best I know how for Him," she said confidently.

"Yes, ma'am, you have," I confirmed.

"So, it's okay if I'm ready to die, right?" Her coy expression made me laugh a bit.

"Ma, you're 75 years old, you have fought a good fight; you are entitled to die, if you want to!" I replied.

"Are you sure?" she asked, a little hesitant.

I responded playfully, but in all seriousness: "Ma, I give you my permission to die!"

"And you and your sisters?" she asked.

"We will be just fine."

The atmosphere in the room lightened up quite a bit as mom continued our conversation. "Well, when I die, I don't want anyone wearing black at my funeral."

"Is that right?" I asked. "What color do you want them to wear?"

"Blue and white. I will be in heaven, rejoicing with my Savior!"

"Indeed, you will be, Mom!" I confirmed. "Is there anything else you would like?"

"Take care of your sisters; don't let them go."

"I won't."

With that said, she continued to gleefully describe how she wanted her funeral to be.

Little did I know that, six months later, she would take me up on my words and choose to go be with the Lord.

To better understand the significance of that special conversation, I will ask that you travel back in time with me for a moment. I believe this is a good place to put in a disclaimer, as I have never fully submerged myself into my native culture, nor returned to visit Haiti since I left as a child. Any reference to Haiti that I speak of here was told to me by my mother and close relatives who lived there. Now, let's journey to the past.

It was December 1970. The little woman waddled into her home after a long day at the hospital. She enjoyed being a nurse, but at eight-and-a-half months pregnant, work could get a tad bit daunting. She sat down to rest, trying to catch her breath; when, right before her eyes, her stomach flattened as if she had never been pregnant or had already given birth. Panicked, the woman called for her sister and father to take her to the hospital. Once there, the doctors were astonished—no movement, no heartbeat, no life. No one had an answer, other than to pray. The woman determinedly brought her petition before the throne of grace and vigorously pleaded for the life of her child.

That woman was my mother, and that child was me.

My mother was a great nurse and worked in one of the top hospitals in Port-au-Prince. While she was working there, my father happened to come to the hospital, saw her, and started to pursue her. When my mother was six years old, her mother and baby sister had died, and she had become the youngest of six children. Not wanting to be a burden to her siblings, she decided to marry my father.

After getting married, they tried and miscarried several times for two years before my mother became pregnant with me at age 30. Sometime during her pregnancy, my father went to the United States to make a new home for his family.

My mother was living with her father and sister when her stomach went flat. The story went something like this: someone did not approve of her marriage to my father and had gone to a voodoo doctor to have their first child killed before being born. Everybody panicked, but my mother pleaded to the Lord for her child's life. They took her to the hospital, and she gave birth to a four-pound baby girl. To my mother, I was her gift; she finally had a little person who would love her unconditionally and a companion to whom she could tell all her secrets. To my father, I was a disappointment; a male child was supposed to open his wife's womb. To everyone else, I was nothing short of a miracle, and the pride and joy of both my grandfathers.

True to her word, my mother started confiding in me while I was still in the crib. She said I was a unique child: quiet and content. I never really cried, and when people came to visit, they didn't know she had a baby in the house unless she told them.

When I turned one, my father sent for my mother, and I was left with my aunt and grandfather. My aunt was like a second mom to me.

When I was four years old, my father sent for me to come rejoin the family. I traveled to Brooklyn, New York with my grandfather (my father's dad). From the moment I saw my father, I was afraid of him. I clung to my grandfather and would not let go. By then, my mother had my little sister. As I watched my little sister interact with my father, I eventually warmed up to him a little, and finally stopped crying and trembling every time he walked into the same room as me.

My mother started to confide in me again. As the oldest, I was a miniature adult with lots of responsibilities. My mother, not knowing the language, was unable to go to school and get her nursing degree; instead, she worked as a home health aide. My grandfather stayed with us for some time to help take care of us while our parents were at work, but he soon left and returned to Haiti.

Two years later, my mother had my next little sister. And when I was ten years old, she got pregnant with our baby sister. At 40 years old, the pregnancy was unexpected and very difficult. My mother ended up having a C-section with complications, and I became her everything. Once my sister was born, I took care of both her and my mother. I continued to help her with my other sisters as well, and I did most of the cooking and the cleaning. I was my mom's "right hand", as she put it.

The older I became, the more I got to know my father, and the more I detested him. As I drew further away from my father, the bond between my mother and me grew stronger.

As early as I can remember, my father used to beat us for the most ignoramus reasons. However, between age 12 and 13, I became acutely aware of his verbal and emotional abuse as well. At the time, I did not know it was abuse; I just knew that he was mean and that I was afraid of him. I despised how he constantly spewed out foul words to make us fear him. I remember specifically being called, "ugly, lazy, nasty, worthless and wouldn't amount up to anything". Nothing I did was ever good enough for him, yet I did everything.

It was also around that age I began to realize that, although we were living in America, we were being raised as Haitians. Two totally different cultures! Also around this age, in addition to the physical, verbal, mental, and emotional abuses, I became acutely aware of being sexually abused. Mind you, I know the terms today and can see what was happening; however, as a 13-year-old Haitian child, I just knew I hated my father and did not like how he made me feel when I was around him. So, I avoided being around him for any reason as much as possible. In all my observations, I also realized my mom was one of us, with absolutely no authority. Later on, I found out that women are considered to be property in Haiti, even to this day.

A lot happened during my childhood; amidst it all, I found myself becoming the protector for both my mother and sisters. The story was that my father's mother did not want him to marry my mother; therefore, she did not accept my mother or her children. So very sad. Whenever my grandmother was around, she instigated trouble for my mother, my sisters, and me. Every time she visited, we were guaranteed to get a beating after she left or sometimes while she was still there. My father once said that he was the king of his castle and we were all his servants, my mother included, and so he could do whatever he wanted. My grandmother supported that!

As time passed, my father seemed to get worse. There are several memories etched in my mind. I will tell of a few that truly set change into motion.

One Sunday after church, the youth met at our house and we were all in the backyard, eating and talking. Everyone was home and some of the church members, whose teens attended, were there too. After they all left, my father called my sister and me into his room and locked the door. We knew we were in trouble, but for what? We had no clue.

He told us how we had embarrassed him by playing around with the boys like a bunch of whores. He said the church members had seen it and thought we were fast. On and on he went. Anyway, the dreaded command finally came: he told us to take off our clothes. That's how we got beat—naked, and forced to watch each other get beat. His rule was that since I was the oldest, I went first. I lay on the bed and literally separated my mind from my body. My father got angry 'cause I wasn't screaming and yelling; I was just grunting. He said I was the child of the devil and he was gonna beat the Hades out of me. I did my best to ignore him, and it finally ended.

Then it was my sister's turn, but she

wasn't so compliant. She tried to run, but my father caught her around the neck and threw her against the dresser. My sister fell to the floor and he began to hit her all over with the leather belt, mainly across her chest and her abdomen. I was screaming and went forward to try and stop him, but he pushed me against the wall. I froze and just stood there stunned, helplessly watching. I didn't know what to do. My mother was home, but she did not come to help. I truly didn't understand. She had to have known something was not right.

That incident scarred me. It was one thing for him to hurt me, but it was an entirely different thing to watch him hurt my sister so brutally. I promised myself at that moment that, whenever possible, I would not let him beat my sisters. I would protect them at whatever cost. And I hated him even more than before.

That summer, we got up one Saturday morning and were told to pack our things. With no forewarning, we moved permanently to New Rochelle, which was a two-hour drive away from Brooklyn.

Although we were not permitted to have friends, we did so in secret, and we did not get a chance to say good-bye. My father had received his ordination as a pastor, and he was assigned to start a new church in New Rochelle. When we got there, he basically ignored us as he worked hard to open up his church before school started.

My mom gave us a little bit of freedom to leave the house. I was curious to know where the new high school was, so my sister and I took the city bus to our new school. When we got there, the summer track team was practicing. We met the coach, who invited me to join the team. I told him I wanted to but had a lot of responsibilities at home, and that I would only be able to make the home games. He agreed.

My parents did not believe in after-school activities or summer school; if you had to participate in any activities after school or during the summer, it meant you were in trouble. I joined the team and kept it a secret from my parents. As the summer progressed, we found different reasons to go visit the school. I continued to secretly run track, and Coach became a good friend. He was easy to get along with and did not push me for any explanations.

By the time school started, for the first time in my life, I was part of something that did not involve the scrutiny of my parents. Once I got my credits evaluated, I found out I had more credits than needed for my grade, so I only had to go to school half a day. I also found out that Coach was not just the track coach, but the school counselor as well. On one occasion, he told me that I was a little too happy and that he had never met anyone as happy as I was—alluding to the fact that something may be wrong. What he didn't know is that what he saw was my public face; my parents had trained us to wear it outside the home. I realized then that he was as observant as I was and decided to be more careful around him.

A few months after school started, the church was flourishing and running smoothly. Besides church, my father had a new job as a cab driver, and my mother had a new job as a home health aide. Sometimes her job required her to be gone overnight.

On one such night, my father called me into his room for the first time since we had moved. He told me to come and let him look at how much I had grown and matured into a woman. I was 16 years old and must have had a growth spurt over the summer; who knows. But he put his hand under my shirt and touched my breasts; he then told me to turn around and commented on how round my buttocks had gotten as he touched them. He put his hand up my skirt and was generally touching me all over. I felt nasty and uncomfortable, but silently followed his commands.

Then he told me to sit on the bed next to him. I sat facing him. He put his hand on my thigh and spoke the words that changed my life forever. He said that if he wasn't married to my mother, he would marry me. Then he said that if something ever happened to my mother, he would make me his wife. I wasn't sure how serious he was. To some, whose father are their heroes, those words would be endearing; but to an abused Haitian girl, that was a death sentence! I decided right there that I would rather be dead than potentially be his wife someday.

Since I only had school for half a day, I would go to the library and do my homework while I waited for my sister. Three days after the incident with my father, I came home after my last class at noon. I sat down and wrote my mother a five-page letter explaining why I did not want to live anymore. I taped the letter to their bedroom door. Then I went into the medicine cabinet and took out the heart meds, high blood pressure meds, and whatever else. I crushed them all up and poured them into a cup. I took a bottle of NyQuil and mixed it all together. I sat on my bed before drinking it and prayed to God.

"God," I began, *"I really don't want to die, but I would rather come be with You instead of someday becoming my father's wife."* Then I told Him what my mother taught us to say, *"Nevertheless, not my will but Yours be done."* Praying that God would understand why I was doing this, I made one last request. *"All I ask, Lord, is that if You let me live, take me away from this hell I'm living in, and I will serve You for the rest of*

my life." After saying the prayer, I stirred the cup and drank it all down. I laid on the bed and went to sleep.

I woke up three weeks later at my aunt's house in Brooklyn.

The story went like this: my parents came home, found the letter, and found me. My father did not allow my mother to take me to the hospital because he did not want his reputation as a pastor to be tarnished. Instead, they took me to my aunt's house for her to nurse me back to health. My aunt had been a nurse in Haiti too, but she said that without any medical equipment, she had no idea what to do. She just cried, fasted, and prayed for God to help her and help me. My aunt was ecstatic when I finally woke up because she said that was the second time God had saved my life. Two weeks after I woke up, I went back home.

You can imagine: I was angry with God. Not only was I back home, but my parents were scrutinizing my every move. They told me the story I was to tell the school principal and anyone else who asked me what happened: "I went to visit and help my aunt because she was very sick".

For the next couple days in school, I avoided Coach. About the third day, he caught up with me in the hallway. He said he hadn't seen me in a while and to please stop by his office after class so we could talk. I reluctantly agreed. I went to his office 30 minutes before school ended, hoping to make our conversation quick. I had to meet up with my sister and go home, or I would be in trouble with my father. I knocked, walked into his office, and sat down on one of the chairs across from his desk. He was sitting there doing paperwork. He stopped and smiled at me as I came in.

"Why did you leave without saying a word?" he asked. "I thought we were friends."

"I'm sorry," was all I could say.

"Plus, you left your teammates short a relay person."

"I'm sorry," I repeated.

"It's okay. We all missed you." He smiled. "So, where did you go?"

I told him the rehearsed story my parents had instructed me to say.

His smile faded. "You know that I know you well enough to know when you're lying, right?" He smiled again and jokingly stated, "Am I going to have to pry the truth out of you?"

I can't explain what happened at that moment in time, but I decided to tell him the truth.

"I tried to kill myself, and they sent me away."

He got up very slowly, came around the desk, and sat on the edge. Then he asked, "So, how did you go about doing that?"

I told him the ugly truth. He then kneeled in front of me, coming down to my level, and asked, "Why would you do such a thing?"

"Because my father hurts me."

"How?" was his simple question.

But I didn't—couldn't say a word.

After a short silence, he asked, "Now that you're back home, are you planning to try again?"

"Yes."

"How?"

"I'm going to take the car, drive down

the street around the corner from our house, and drive off the cliff."

He slowly got up, walked to the door, and locked it with a key.

I panicked and asked, "What are you doing? I have to get home!"

He calmly stated, "I can't let you leave my office." He came back to where I was sitting and now crying, and resumed his kneeling position. He took my hands.

"I'm not going to leave you alone. I'm going to help you."

No one had ever said that to me before.

He asked again, "How does your father hurt you?"

I finally broke down and told him that he beat us and touched my private areas.

He then explained in great detail how he was going to call CPS and have them go to the house to talk to my parents. He explained what CPS was and what they were going to do to help. Still in a haze, I nodded my understanding.

He asked me what time my parents were coming home. I told him. I also told him I needed to talk to my sisters before anyone came home. He said he would take me home about ten minutes before my parents came home, and he would tell CPS to be there at least five minutes after they arrived. He also said he would be outside the whole time until CPS took us away.

After making all the necessary calls and arrangements, he did as he said and took me home ten minutes before my parents were due. I rushed in and spoke to my sisters, who were already panicking because I had missed the bus. I told them what I had done; they weren't happy about it, but they weren't too upset either.

Almost as soon as I finished speaking to them, my parents came through the door. We were in our room; my heart was pounding, and I didn't know what to do. Before we could even go out to face my parents, the doorbell rang, and it was CPS. We heard them talking for a little bit, and then my mother called me. My sisters went out with me (except for our baby sister—she was six, and they had picked her up from daycare on their way home).

As soon as I came out, I saw the CPS

worker and my parents sitting in the living room. I could not meet their eyes. The CPS worker asked me if my father ever spanked me; I said yes. She asked me if I had tried to kill myself; I nodded. She asked me if my father had ever touched my private area; I nodded.

It was then my mother started screaming at me in Creole. She said, "What are you doing? You're destroying our family. Tell them you're lying, tell them nothing like that ever happened."

I looked at her, and all emotion left me. She was holding and rocking my little sister, who was now crying. This was the woman I had been loyal to for all these years—whose secrets I had kept—whom I had tried to protect—whom I would have given my life for, and here she was, telling me to protect the very man who hurt me over and over again.

I dared not look at my father. He was silent the whole time, but I could feel his gaze boring into me.

Then the CPS lady said to my mom, "Ma'am, you have to make a decision: either your husband needs to leave the home, or we will have to take the kids".

My mom's next words tore into my very soul as she said, "Take the kids."

I was glad I was emotionally numb, because if I could have felt anything at that moment, I would have been enraged. They dragged my little sister, kicking and screaming, from my mother's arms and out the door. My mother was still screaming at me in Creole, telling me how I had just destroyed the family, and that I was selfish and did not care about anyone but myself. As I was leaving, my father and I briefly locked eyes; the evil I saw there made me decide that I would never again grace his home.

As we went out to the car, I saw Coach sitting in his car. He had stayed true to his word. He drove off as we left.

As we drove away, I held my crying sisters tight. I had blown it. The CPS lady went straight to the hospital and I found myself alone in the psych ward under suicide watch. I felt so alone and miserable; all that kept replaying in my head was my mother saying "Take the kids" and accusing me of destroying the family. I just wanted to die. I had messed up big time by telling Coach. I broke the rule: *"What happens in this house, stays in this house. You don't tell strangers family secrets."* And I was paying dearly for it.

I did not eat or sleep for about two or three days. I just cried. They finally had to sedate me. Coach did not leave me alone; he came to visit and brought me homework, which kept me distracted. He told me that my two younger sisters were back home, but my 14-year-old sister did not want to go back, so she was placed in a foster home.

Coach consistently came to visit, although I didn't have much to say anymore. I had betrayed my family; I wasn't going to continue to do so.

After spending 30 days in the psych ward, I was taken to a foster home. I wanted to be with my sister, but they wouldn't let me. A friend of mine had an aunt who had retired from being a foster mom, but she came out of retirement to take me in. I returned to school and continued with track.

I joined the Army Delayed Entry Program. My intent behind joining the Army was to learn how to shoot a gun so I could come back and kill my father.

A year and half later, I finished high school. Although I invited my family to the graduation, not one of them showed up, and I'm sure it was my father's doing. I asked my father to sign the papers to let my 16-year-old sister, who was now living in a group home, become my dependent in the Army, but he refused. Before I left, I made sure she was transferred to my old foster home; at least I knew she would be safe there. Less than a week after I graduated, I left for basic training.

Afterwards, God made sure I would not be able to kill my father by sending me to Germany for my first duty station. While in Germany, I rededicated my life to the Lord and started serving Him with all my heart. It was also there that I met and married my husband of 27 years, and we traveled the world.

I never lost contact with my mother. In fact, as time went on, I realized that God had answered my prayer. Years later, I was able to forgive both of my parents, but never lived near them.

As my parents' health started to fail over the years, I traveled back and forth to New York to see about them. While stationed in Washington state in 2014, we found out that my mother had lung cancer. Again, God orchestrated things. My husband got ordered to Fort Bragg, and we moved to North Carolina in April 2016. Due to the extent of their health issues, my parents moved here in June 2016, and I became their primary caregiver.

Mind you, I had not been around my father for any real length of time since I was 16 years old; so, a lot of old feeling creeped in, and we were toxic around each other. He had never acknowledged he did anything wrong and continued to blame me for messing up his life. He was never held accountable for what he did, because all charges were dropped due to my mother's testimony.

Anyway, they moved into an apartment about ten minutes away from our house. My mother was in and out of the hospital, and she had to have bypass surgery in her leg due to diabetes. After the surgery, she was placed in a nursing home to recover. While she was there, my father went to New Jersey to visit with his family. He stayed there for four months. It was during this time that my mother and I were able to bond again on a deeper level. We talked a lot about everything and did a lot of fun things together. She was a totally different woman when my father wasn't around, fun and carefree.

Over the years, she confided in me that she wanted to leave him several times; but, due to cultural and religious beliefs that God did not allow divorce under any circumstances, especially with a pastor's wife, she dutifully stayed.

My mom's favorite movies were *Sister Act* and *Sister Act 2*. I used to lie in the nursing home bed next to her, and we would binge on *Sister Act*. One day, after watching the first *Sister Act*, Mom stated, "Nanoune, do you know why I love *Sister Act* so much?"

I said, "No, ma'am."

She continued, "Because Deloris knows how to protect herself and others."

That spoke volumes to me. She was telling me she wished she could have protected herself and us. She then apologized, for the umpteenth time, for not being there for me when I needed her the most. I told her all was already forgiven.

She took my hands and said, "Nanoune, God is so awesome."

I responded, "He surely is."

Then she said, "Look what God has done."

She paused for moment. I waited for her to continue, and she did.

"He took you and put you in the Army— made you a captain, well respected and able to command. He made you strong. But to keep you humble and from being prideful, He made you a nurse—where you were able to identify with those who were suffering and help them. He made you compassionate. Then He made you a counselor—where you are able to understand people, and give guidance. He made you wise. God is awesome: He gave you strength, compassion, and wisdom."

She paused again.

I thought to myself, *Only Mom could come up with such a correlation.*

Then she said, "I'm very proud of you."

Those words broke me. When I left to join the Army at 18, I was considered a rebel and was blamed for breaking up the family. To hear those words coming from my mom was a healing balm. And I was grateful to God for giving us this precious time together.

So, now, we're back to where we started. I gave my mom permission to die in peace. Mom left the nursing home in February 2017 and was doing extremely well when she got out. The doctors predicted a full recovery and said she would be back to her old self in no time. The lung cancer was slow-growing and would not affect her daily life; however, they would continue to monitor it. With that piece of good news, she went home.

Mom and I came to our very first King's Daughters meeting together in February.

She fell in love with Ms. Deborah. She was excited and told me how she loved the women and couldn't wait to come back the next month. My father had returned from New Jersey, and we were looking for a Baptist church for them to call home. For all intents and purposes, she was on the road to recovery fast.

However, a couple of weeks later, she started sleeping a lot, and I took her to the emergency room. They diagnosed her with unexpected respiratory failure due to the lung cancer. The doctors said she could fight it, but she did not want to. She never returned home.

On her death bed, in that hospital room, she had more strength, wisdom, dignity, and control over her life than she ever had in her whole entire life. She summoned all her daughters to her. We were and are still affectionately called "Mommy's Girls". My sisters came from New York and Texas with their children. Mom gave her daughters instructions to be there for each other. She kissed her grandchildren and great-grandkids. Then she asked for the breathing tube to be removed. She drew her last breath and died peacefully, with her family surrounding her. I believe God gave her that gift: to make the final decision on when she would come meet Him. I also believe my mother gave up her life to free me from my father. She made the ultimate sacrifice of laying down her life.

My mother was the epitome of what it means to love others—friends and foes alike. Everyone who met her was attracted to her, and she was always telling them about the love of Jesus through her words and actions. As a child, there were a lot of things I did not understand. But as an adult, I can see how hard it would have been to leave your spouse while living in a foreign country with no citizenship, trying to navigate in a culture that you didn't even know or understand, with four young children. I learned a lot from My Mom: how to trust God in everything, and how to never give up, and how to humbly ask for forgiveness, and how to forgive—regardless of how difficult.

I am who I am today by the grace of God; He came through for me when I needed Him most! He mended my broken heart and shattered life. He renewed the relationship between my mother and me, and for that, I'll forever be grateful. Today, I choose to be an advocate for those who do not have a voice, because I understand the importance of having someone stand by you when you can't stand alone. Despite all that I suffered as a child, I daily choose to be a victor and not a victim. I am married to a wonderful, godly man, and we have four beautiful children and two adorable grandkids! I love life! I enjoy life!

AMY BLOUNT

I know there are many parents who have struggled, will struggle, or are now in that struggle of wanting their child/children to be obedient and not stray away from God, yet they have found themselves crying out to God for help concerning those children. I will share my story of heartbreak, disappointment, uncertainty, confusion, offense, and then the Victory that God has promised to those who will trust and obey Him. Those who believe and not doubt that whatsoever they ask of God in Jesus' name according to His will, He will do it for those who will count HIM faithful to fulfill HIS promises. **God Is faithful!**

I am the mother of five very different children, and the grandmother of three grand-beauties who have their own ways of being in this world. The child that I will be sharing about is my oldest. She was always the goal-oriented, focused, ambitious type— very smart, and she used good common sense. I used to pray and ask God to keep her as His, because if she ever turned away from Him, she would lead a lot of people to hell.

This may sound strange or even arrogant, but it's neither—not if you understand people, their gifts, and how the devil wants to use them. I noticed things about her when she was just an infant/toddler that fascinated and frightened me at the same time; things she would say or do, or behaviors she'd express that weren't typical of most children her age—well, that I had been around. I could discern that she was a leader, from a very young age.

I'll share a little bit of my background as *her* mother. I did not grow up in a Christian home, where mom and dad took the children to church. I did, however, get born again when I was about seven years old, via a street ministry. My mother, who was single most of the time, would go to church on certain occasions, but not regularly. She would send me and my siblings, or we'd catch rides to church service. Years later, my mother began to go regularly to the church we attended, but I'll save the details of that story for another time.

Many changes occurred from my

childhood to my teenage years, and more through my young adult years. I did eventually make my way into a loving fellowship with God. I met up and began a great friendship with a youth pastor and his wife, Pastor Windle and Eliza Riles. They were amazing mentors from God in my life—we're still friends today. I took one last turn down a dark path for about two years when I was 17; this detour lasted until I was 19. I ended up away from God, pregnant, and not married.

When I truly repented and got back into fellowship with the Lord, my life changed drastically, and I've not turned back since. I knew how important it would be for me to not allow my child to born into a cursed—generationally cursed—situation. I just wasn't going to allow it! I got out of a sinful situation and vowed that my daughter would be blessed, and that she would not carry this behavior into her future.

While I was carrying her, I prayed and read the Scriptures to her daily, throughout the day. I was determined to fill her with the Word even before she got here. I wanted to ensure that she would be free of any generational curses—free to love and serve God with all her might. When she was born, I continued what I had started. We prayed and were in the Word daily.

As she began walking and talking, she did everything early: crawling at 4 months, walking at 7 months, and talking about that age! By the time she was three years old, she could answer most of the questions to enroll herself into preschool. She could read 3 to 5-word sentences as we were passing billboards. God had blessed us, and I wanted to remain there, in that place of blessing, so that she could see by example the benefits of being a child of God—being in fellowship with and serving HIM.

Fast forwarding many years later, I'm now married with four more children. My oldest was the only child not biologically my husband's. He accepted her and asked many times to adopt her. He didn't want her to have a different last name or feel separate from the others. We were going through life as many families do.

I began to notice a difference in her

attitude and behavior when she got into 7th grade. By 8th grade, she was becoming rebellious and rude at home and to others in authority—teachers and such. She was not happy at all! She didn't have a choice whether to go to church or not, as we did when I was growing up. So, she went—but not joyfully. She still did much of what was required at home, but her talking back disrespectfully and challenging almost everything offended me and her dad quite often. She has a very strong personality that can be intimidating or just offensive to most people until they get to know her. Imagine dealing daily with this and the atmosphere it set, and trying to handle things from a godly perspective.

I prayed all the time about her, us, and her relationship with others, especially my husband. This period in our lives was so hard, so uncomfortable . . . just despicable. I would frequently pray the Word, straight from the Word, over us and over her individually. Yet, situations seemed to grow worse.

While I loved my daughter and wanted

to be there for her, I was still offended and angry because of the rude and rebellious way she behaved. Most of the time, I wanted to grab her and love on her, because I knew something was wrong. I didn't know if she was just going through that teenage stage of acquiring autonomy, or if it was something more. Some days, I just couldn't get past the rude and disrespectful things she would do. I tried to see life from her perspective, as our household was far from perfect. We were both dealing with a lot of hurt and disappointment coming from many different sources. I just didn't know how deeply hurt and confused she was.

I realized I was expecting her to be a Christian adult about things when she was just a child. But for a while, it didn't matter that I realized my expectations were too much at the time. I was offended and had let that offense take root in me, which only made conditions worse! I began to act very indifferent towards her and her needs.

I had started rehearsing the lies she was telling, and I was upset that she was doing foolish things that cost us chunks of money.

Every time she'd do something new, I would recall all the previous things done, and this would just fuel my reasons for justifying why I didn't need to be sympathetic concerning her issues, because *"She knows better"* and *"She's just being mean"*!

During the time all of this was in progress, I was a youth leader; I was on the prayer team; I was involved with the women's' ministry and whatever else I chose to help out with. I kept myself as clean as I thought I could by repenting daily, spending time in God's Word/presence, and caring for my family as best I knew how, yet things escalated in the wrong direction. One of the most disturbing occurrences was seeing some lyrics my husband showed me. He'd found gospel songs with vulgar lyrics mixed in . . . it was, indeed, my daughter's handwriting. I didn't know what to say about it, so I didn't say much at all.

All this time, I was literally crying out to God about this situation. My husband was trying to deal with it the only way he knew how; things were very tense in our home, and for many reasons. But these episodes made life almost unbearable. Dealing with them both, dealing with one another—some days, it was too much! My husband took her bedroom door off at one time. Then, eventually, he told her to get out of the house. She left without saying where she was going. I later found out where she'd been staying and had her come back home, especially when I saw whom she was staying with.

My daughter was getting into squabbles with other kids, and one such incident almost got her arrested. She even busted out a window at school, saying it was accidental. I remember one day, after she got home from school, my front yard filled up with teenagers who were yelling for her to come out and fight. I then found out that a few of the girls had planned to jump her when she got off the bus that day. Apparently, things didn't go as planned.

The worst part about this is that a parent, one of the girl's moms, joined the crowd that came to my house to help fight my daughter. Also, one of the girls had a stapler tied on string that she was planning to use to beat my daughter. Even sadder, the girl who had the stapler was the one my daughter stayed with when she left our house. (*I had warned my daughter about that girl when I met her.*) I was sympathetic then and wanted to get ugly with the crowd, especially that mom, but I chose the wiser route. We lived on post at the time, so I called the MPs (military police), filing yet another police report concerning my daughter.

One day, I was standing in my kitchen, looking out the window. I began to ask the Lord what I was missing. I asked HIM to tell me what my part was in all of this. Again, I asked, *"Father God, in Jesus' name, what do YOU want me to do? What is my part?"* I said, *"I know I'm not supposed to feel this way about my own child . . . but I don't like her! YOU already know what's in my heart, and I can't stand her right now! I just want her out! If I could, I would cut her off completely! I can't get Reg to commit to praying and fasting with me to break this bondage. I feel like I'm in a whirlwind. I know I'm not supposed to feel this way about my own daughter, about my family— my God, I feel miserable about it all! Lord, what do YOU want me to do?"*

As I stood there, looking out the window, waiting for an answer, I heard in my spirit—like in my gut, then in my head— **"40 days."**

It was not a loud or audible voice, but it was clear and distinguishable, so I repeated what I heard and asked, *"40 days?"*

And there was a confirmation: **"Yes, 40 days."**

I went to my bookshelf and pulled out a little book that I had bought about two years prior. I read the title out loud: *"Speak the Word Over Your Family for Salvation,* by Harry and Cheryl Salem." I flipped through the pages slowly this time, reading the words, and said, "These are the Scriptures I've been praying, and many more, all laid out for 40 days." The Holy Spirit knew then, when He prompted me to buy *that* book, that I would use it, just as I'd prophesied when I said, "I'll need this one day" as I tossed it in my basket with other books.

I didn't wait; I began that same day. I

was serious and expectant, still not fully appreciative of what had just happened. God had heard my sincere cry, and He had seen my repentant heart about feeling the way I felt, and He answered me. He told me *my part* to do as He included me in His solution—one that was about to make manifest a miracle!

I kept daily notes and was amazed on some of those days. On the third day, my daughter came into the house and stood at the kitchen entrance, a few feet across from where I was standing. There was a child's gate at the entrance. She asked me to come to her; and, being that I was still unaware of how deep the stinky offense was rooted, I said, "No, you come to me."

She said, "Ok, then I'll come to you."

Now, this was not her typical behavior at all! Normally, she would have said "Forget it" and walked away, but not this time. She walked over to me, apologized for her past behavior and bad attitude, and asked if this could be a new start for us.

I was shocked, happy, and ashamed at the same time! She hugged me first; I halfway hugged her back, when I should have embraced her with everything in me, but I couldn't. See, I needed deliverance too. That was day *three*, y'all!

Day ten fell on a Sunday. We went to church service, as usual. My daughter sat next to me and held her head down in her lap for most of the service. I wanted to tell her to sit up, and I started to, but this thought came rushing in: *"Just leave her alone; she can hear"*—so I left her alone. Towards the end of the sermon, she sat up and said, "When the pastor gives the altar call, will you go up there with me?" (*Can we pause right here for a HalleluJAH!!*) I gave a calm "Yes, of course."

When the call began, she was one of the first to stand. We walked out of the row, with her behind me. I said, "You go ahead, and I will follow you." As she walked to the front of that stage, she broke down, doubled over, and started crying so hard that I was, again, in shock. I didn't know if I should even touch her! We ended up on the far right, about three rows from the stage, as there were many who'd answered the call to salvation.

The pastor walked to the area where we were standing, and he stopped. He paused there for a moment, looked into the audience, and said, "The Lord said this is a new start for some of you."

Again, I'm in awe of my God! He's so personal in His compassion and great grace towards us. Remember my daughter's request for a new start on day *three*? God, in His loving kindness, confirmed the new start *seven* days later. She repented, confessed Jesus as Lord, and was born again that day!! Of course, it was ON for those next 30 days!

Some changes were immediate; others, God graced us to work through. My heart was softening again, and the Lord was showing me how offense had taken my compassion and empathy away. I was not as discerning, and I was halfhearted about His Kingdom business. The Lord spoke to me about my behavior and how it was keeping me from genuine intimate fellowship with Him. I was not strong anymore in the Spirit, even though the anger was making me feel strong. I learned how deceived we can become when offense is allowed to take root and grow.

We joined a church during this time, and she went on a camping trip with the youth—something she would not have agreed to prior to her salvation experience. On the way back from the trip, my daughter called me while still on the bus. She was so excited about what had happened to her. My daughter said that while she and the youth director were praying, she heard chains falling to the ground. She said, "I heard clanging, like they were hitting the ground. It was so loud that I opened my eye to see if chains were on the ground." It made me so happy to hear how excited she was about godly things and what He was doing in her life.

I would love to say that life was perfect after the 40 days, but it wasn't. I can praise God, however, for ALL the goodness that came out of those 40 days of prayer. The Lord showed Himself *faithful*, kind, longsuffering, patient, and loving. He is so good!

Incidentally, the number 40 is a

number of probation/ testing/ trial, ending in victory or defeat.

My daughter is now a married woman with a great husband. They met in basic military training, got married at their first duty station, have two children, and are getting ready to celebrate their tenth wedding anniversary. She is a youth leader at her church and has some great accomplishments under her belt with her military career. I'm so proud of her, and I love her so very much!!

I want to leave you with God's Word: the sword He's given us to cut the enemy completely out of our lives. Always use the same strategy Jesus used—IT IS WRITTEN!

Jeremiah 1:12 (AMPC)
"Then said the Lord to me, You have seen well, for I am alert and active, watching over My word to perform it."

Psalm 46:1 (NLT)
"God is our refuge and strength, always ready to help in times of trouble."

Psalm 46:1 (AMP)
*"God is our refuge and strength
[mighty and impenetrable],
A very present and well-proved help
in trouble."*

Romans 10:13 (NLT)
*"For 'Everyone who calls on the name of
the Lord will be saved.'"*

John 6:37 (AMP—emphasis added)
*"'All that My Father gives Me will come to
Me; **and the one who comes to Me I
will most certainly not cast out [I
will never, never reject anyone who
follows Me].'"***

Philippians 1:6 (AMP)
*"I am convinced and confident of this very
thing, that He who has begun a good work
in you will [continue to] perfect and
complete it until the day of Christ Jesus
[the time of His return]."*

You see, it all begins with the Lord, and
it all ends with Him. Our part is to simply:
Seek, Trust, and Obey.

DEBORAH WALLACE

Redeeming Love

"I never want to get married again!"

These were the words I spoke to the Lord approximately two decades ago, after He informed me that there would be no reconciliation in my marriage. How could this be? I had prayed, interceded, and believed that God would heal our broken vows. I trusted God to mend the fragmented pieces of a love that was supposed to endure "till death do us part". Yet, He told me that all my praying, believing, and trusting were for naught—nothing.

"Why, Lord? Why won't you help me? Why won't You do a miracle in my husband's heart?"

I had been in what felt like a loveless marriage for years, experiencing the disappointment, pain, anguish, heartbreak, and heartache of the worst betrayal. As loveless as the marriage felt, I still held onto hope for a miracle, not realizing the miracle that was needed was for my own heart. I needed the courage and strength to accept what the Lord had spoken to me. With tears flowing and heart broken, I told Abba: *"I never want to get married again!"*

He gently told me that I would indeed marry again, and that I would know what it is to be loved by a godly man. He also spoke these words to me: *"You are not allowed to date."* The Lord said that my promised marriage would not be about the pursuit of happiness; it would be about the plans and purposes of God. He said the happiness and joy I would experience would be the fringe benefits of being in a kingdom marriage.

Not allowed to date. What man is going to marry me without dating me?

The Lord told me that my husband would know that I was to be his wife by the Holy Spirit, and that I would know my husband in the same way. I said to the Lord, *"Okay, but if I am to marry again, You are going to have to do it."*

On this journey of marriage, I have learned some things. Although God is all knowing—He knows whom we will eventually marry—He gives us the choice. God will bring a man and woman together for the purpose of marriage, but He will not force them to marry, because He has given all of us free will. Many have missed out on a good, godly spouse, holding out for someone they considered BETTER while failing to realize that the BEST was right in front of them.

Please understand: this is my story. It is not intended to be legalistic about dating or courting. God told me that I was not allowed to date; that does not mean He will speak the same to you. Our heavenly Father, Abba, really does know best. We must trust this.

"Alright, Lord," I told Him. *"If I am to marry again, I want to experience marriage and sex according to Your Word, Your Will, and Your Way, Yahweh!"*

During the waiting, there was much work to be done within me to prepare me for this fulfilled promise of a kingdom marriage. Philippians 1:6 reminds us that God has begun a good work in us and that He will complete it. I have given Him a lot to work with. It took almost twenty years for God to prepare me for His son: my husband.

For those who have been married and

are now separated or divorced, you know that once you have experienced the touch of a spouse (read between the lines here), it can be a challenge once that touch is no longer available. I was determined that I would experience marriage and sex as purposed by God Almighty. I prayed and asked Him to be Lord over my passions, and He faithfully answered that prayer during those years of waiting. He kept me because **I wanted to be kept** sexually pure. I did not have sexual intercourse until the fulfilled promise of the godly husband and godly marriage, on our wedding night. Nevertheless, if any have fallen into sexual immorality, know that repentance and forgiveness are available, and that God is willing and able to keep you if you want to be kept.

I did try to help Him out a time or two (or three) with the dating, always with great disappointment. I thought, *"Maybe he is the one"* or *"That is the one"*, only to experience even more disappointment and betrayal. After my third round of *"This is the one"*, I told myself, *"That's it; no more. I am waiting on the promise of my husband to be fulfilled as the Lord told me: my husband will know me—and I him—by the Spirit of God."*

Through the years of singleness, much took place in my oneness with the Lord and in my spiritual growth. There was much breaking, refashioning, and molding. Christ was being formed in me in ways I had not realized were needed. For example, I was in need of healing and deliverance from ungodly mindsets about myself. I had to learn that my value was not based on people's opinion of me, but rather on the price that Christ Jesus paid for me. Neither my past nor the opinion of man would be allowed to define me any longer. My prayers changed. I began to yield even more, surrendering to the sovereignty of the Holy Spirit and allowing Him to do what only He could do in my heart and soul.

From time to time, I would meditate on the promise of my godly husband. There were hard questions to be answered. One day, while I was out with one of my sisters in Christ, a gentleman walked by us. My sister looked at me and asked if I thought he could be her Boaz. The Lord spoke to me and said, *"She is asking the wrong question. The question she should ask is: 'Am I a Ruth worthy of a Boaz?'."* That resounded in my spirit. I asked myself: *"Am I a Ruth worthy of a Boaz? Why should God entrust His son to me?"* My prayer concerning my husband was for God to make me a Ruth worthy of a Boaz.

I asked God to teach me what a marriage made in heaven—true holy matrimony—looked like through His eyes, as He intended the covenant of marriage to be in His Word. I also told Abba that I wanted to be so content in Him that when the time came for me to marry, He would say, *"Daughter, it is time"*, and I would say, *"Daddy, do I have to?"*

Finally, I got to the place of contentment where if it were to be just Jesus and me for the rest of my life, it was alright with me. This had been a Philippians 3 season of forgetting what was behind, looking forward to what was ahead, and taking hold of that for which Christ Jesus had taken hold of me in order to obtain the fulfilled promise: the prize. What I learned most during this season was that **the process *was* the prize.** Many times, when we fail to embrace the season that God has us in, we forfeit the work that He desires to do—work that must take place within us before it can manifest outside us. I learned much about my God and myself during these years. God did a work in me that no man can take from me.

And then ***suddenly*** . . .

In the beginning of 2019, the Lord told me that I was entering a season of ***suddenly***. As I shared this word with a couple of sisters in Christ during lunch, one of the sisters stopped me and gave me what I did not realize at the time was a prophetic word. She told me that she saw a ring on my finger, and that I was getting ready to get married. Remember, I had finally reached a place of contentment with "just Jesus and me" for the rest of my life; therefore, I gave no credence to what she spoke to me.

Later, as I spoke with another sister in Christ on the phone, she told me of a dream she had had about me. In the dream, there was a gentleman who told me not to worry about anything—just focus on ministry, and he would take care of everything. I gave no credence to this dream either.

And then **suddenly** . . .

After a Thursday Bible study, the Lord told me to go with a sister wherever she was going. I asked her what her plans were for after our class. She told me she was headed to BJ's. I thought, *"Lord, I do not need anything from BJ's; nevertheless, Lord, at Your Word . . ."* (Luke 5:5). While in BJ's, this sister and I were listening to one of the store's product demonstrators, and I saw a gentleman from the corner of my eye. I thought I recognized him from a church I had attended in the late '90s. Out loud, I spoke, "Is that . . .?" (I could not remember his name.) He nodded: "Yes—Mike." (He did not remember my name either.) We only knew each other by face, because the church had been a large congregation. We exchanged pleasantries and contact information.

He called me the next day, Friday, to catch up on what had happened in our lives in the past twenty years. I mentioned to him that I had written a book. He asked me if he could pick up a copy of my book on Saturday. I told him yes, and we made plans for him to do so. When he came to pick the book up, as we engaged in light conversation, he **suddenly** had this profoundly serious look on his face. He looked at me and asked if I were to be his wife. I replied, "If that is the Lord's will, yes."

After he left, I realized I had told this man—whom I had encountered just a couple of days before—that I would marry him. I got scared. The next day, Sunday, when he called, I told him that I thought it best if we were just friends: sister and brother in Christ. He respected my decision.

The Lord led me on a three-day fast. During the fast, the Lord revealed things to me about this gentleman. Some things that He revealed made me skeptical. God told me that just as He had said *"It is good"* when He created the world, He was saying *"It is good"* concerning me and this gentleman—but I had to be willing. God told me that He brings his sons and daughters together for the purpose of marriage, but does not force marriage on us; He has given us free will to decide about every aspect of our lives.

God told me that if I chose to marry Michael, I needed to embrace everything about this brother in Christ—just like He, God Almighty, embraced everything about me. I said, *"Lord, You have shown me some things that I am not sure I want to deal with."*

The Lord asked me a question—and when God asks a question, it is not because He has a need for information. He asked me, *"How much time needs to pass after repentance and forgiveness before you can live as though you have been forgiven?"*

"No time," I responded. *"When I am forgiven, I can stand before You without condemnation, inferiority, or shame, as though the sin never took place."*

The love and forgiveness of our Abba God . . . what manner of love is this! To love as Jesus loves and forgive as He forgives— Lord, help me to be like you!

It was at this moment that I made the choice to move forward in this relationship, if Michael wanted the same. I resolved that I would continually seek to see and understand Michael through the eyes of God.

Michael continued to visit me, and we enjoyed getting to know each other. As the weeks passed by, I began to tell him things about me that I thought would surely turn him off. Yet, no matter what I said, he always responded, "We can work on that" or "We can work through it". No matter what I said, he was not deterred. I began to think, *"He reminds me of someone. What manner of love is this, that this man is so determined that I am the one for him?"*

I said something in reference to my size (I am plus size), and he interrupted. Looking at me intently, he said, **"I see you."**

Michael's words seemed to permeate to the very core of my being. He saw *"Me"*. He saw the treasure of *"Me"* that exists beyond the physical realm. I realized that his love for me reminded me of the redeeming love of God. God is love—constant, unconditional love.

Within weeks of Michael and I running into each other at BJ's, we chose to embrace this supernatural love. Michael officially proposed to me, on bended knee, during a Bible study class at a church called Covenant Love. It was March 20, 2019—National Proposal Day. We are both in our sixties, and we feel greatly blessed that our Lord brought us together in our latter years.

There is much to share about Michael's and my one-flesh union, holy matrimony, but that will come in the book *Redeeming Love*. For now, I leave you with this important lesson I have learned through the years: do it God's way, and you'll get God's results! Believe me, Michael was well worth the two decades of preparation and waiting. We just stare at each other sometimes, in awe of what our Lord did for us in blessing us with each other.

In conclusion, I encourage you—my sister, my brother—that if holy matrimony is what you desire, stay the course of letting your desires be fulfilled through the Word, Will, and Way of Yahweh. Know this: when that special someone comes into your life, he or she will **see you** and appreciate the treasure within. It will be worth the wait. Remember this regarding ALL your desires:

*"Do it God's way
and get God's results!"*

Love and Blessings!

www.ingramcontent.com/pod-product-compliance
Lightning Source LLC
LaVergne TN
LVHW041221080426
835508LV00011B/1023